WHAT'S GREAT ABOUT THIS?

HOW TO BE RESILIENT AND THRIVE
THROUGH DISRUPTION AND CHANGE

BY

DOMINIC SIOW

WHAT'S GREAT ABOUT THIS?

HOW TO BE RESILIENT AND THRIVE THROUGH DISRUPTION AND CHANGE

This book is licensed for your personal enjoyment and education only. While best efforts have been used, the author and publisher are not offering legal, accounting, or any other professional services advice and make no representations or warranties of any kind and assume no liabilities of any kind with respect to the accuracy or completeness of the contents.

All rights reserved. No part of this publication may be reproduced or transmitted in any form or by any means, electronic or mechanical, including photocopying, recording, or by any information storage and retrieval system, without permission in writing from the publisher.

Copyright © 2017 Dominic Siow

QUANTITY PRINT ON DEMAND ORDERS

All titles by international best selling author Dominic Siow are available at special quantity discounts for bulk purchases to be included for: marketing, promotions, fundraisers, and/or educational purposes.

Contact us at info@eqstrategist.com to discuss how we can accommodate your needs.

Or visit our website at: https://www.eqstrategist.com
P O Box 258, Roseville, NSW 2069, Australia

Disclaimer, Please Read

The people and events described and depicted in this book are for educational purposes only. While every attempt has been made to verify the information provided in this book, the author assumes no responsibility for any errors, inaccuracies or omissions.

If advice concerning legal or related matters is needed, the services of a qualified professional should be sought. This book is not intended for use as a source of legal or financial advice. You should be aware of any laws, which govern any financial and business transactions or other business practices in your state.

The examples within this book are not intended to represent or guarantee that everyone or anyone will achieve their desired results. Each individual's success will be determined by his or her desire, dedication, effort and motivation. There are no guarantees that you will achieve your desired outcome. The tools, stories and information are provided as examples only, not as a source of legal or financial advice. You should be aware that any business endeavour has inherent risk for loss of capital.

First Edition 2017 | Copyright © 2017 by Dominic Siow

All rights reserved. No part of this book may be reproduced, stored in a retrieval system, or transmitted in any form by an electronic, mechanical, photocopying, recording means, or otherwise without prior written permission of the publisher, Dominic Siow.

ISBN 9780648018605_0-00

RECOGNITIONS & AWARDS

Keynote Speaking, Training, Coaching and Consulting Services by Dominic Siow can be viewed at http://www.eqstrategist.com/services.html

P O Box 258, Roseville, NSW 2069, Australia

Email: info@eqstrategist.com

DEDICATIONS

For Dad, Mum and Gary, my models of resilience
Jem, Aaron and Courtney, my inspiration for this book
And to my dearest dear, Sue, whose unconditional love made this possible.

To your success, Dominic Siow

"The quality of your life is in direct proportion to the amount of uncertainty that you can comfortably live with."
— Tony Robbins

TABLE OF CONTENTS

Prelude ix
CHAPTER 1 Let's Get Started 1
CHAPTER 2 Disruption and Change – the New Norm 11
CHAPTER 3 How your EQ Affects your Resilience 37
CHAPTER 4 Be the Change.. 63
CHAPTER 5 How Resilient People Move 83
CHAPTER 6 How Resilient People Talk 123
CHAPTER 7 How Resilient People Think................................ 139
CHAPTER 8 How Resilient People Act.................................. 173
CHAPTER 9 Epilogue – Putting it all together 219
Acknowledgements 231
About the Author... 237
References... 243

PRELUDE

*"The future has many names. For the weak, it's unattainable.
For the fearful, it's unknown. For the bold, it's ideal."*
— Victor Hugo

I remember the moment as if it were yesterday. A beautiful, bright, spring Friday morning in Sydney, at 7.30 am, October 2001 to be exact. I answered my phone to a terse voice.

"Dom, is that you?" The voice was Keith, my Asia-Pacific boss. My boss's boss. He was calling from Singapore, and it was 4.30 am there. Hmm. It was the first time I'd ever received a call from him, and a call at that hour made me feel uneasy.

"Yes, it is, Keith. What can I do for you?" I replied, trying to mask my discomfort.

"Dom, I wanted to let you know first-hand that I've decided to restructure your organisation. You're losing 30% of your team today."

It was the call that would alter the course of my life, forever. Until then, my life had been on autopilot. Australian university degree – checked. Job – checked. Car – checked. Settle down – checked! First home – checked. Kids – Checked! Checked! Checked! Promotion to senior role – checked!

Move to chosen neighbourhood for kids' schools – checked. Identify private school for kids – checked!

My path to that stage had pretty much been scripted by my traditional Malaysian upbringing. My parents are Malaysian, of Chinese heritage, and both came from modest backgrounds. Both were also teachers and the kind of people who never had the means to get to university. Not because they didn't have the smarts - they just didn't come from one of *those* families.

Growing up, I remember them often saying to their four sons: "We have no money or business to leave behind for you. All we can do is give you the best education we can afford. Get that overseas university degree and your life is going to be better than ours. The rest is up to you." Their dream was to see four sons through university education in Australia. It was their Everest.

All my life, I was conditioned to strive to achieve. It was my moral duty, as a filial son, to do all I could to use the gifts I was given, to study hard, realise my highest potential through my grades at school, and then get the most prestigious job I could to bring about financial security and status. Achievement would go hand-in-hand with happiness.

I was bookish and always in the "A" class academically (unlike in Australia, schooling in Malaysia back then was streamed – the students with the highest grades were in the A class, the next highest in B, etc.). My life outside of school revolved around the sport of badminton, and I represented my home state in various age groups, at the open level for two years.

I was introverted, shy, loved people, and yet felt socially awkward. As a youth, I led a sheltered life. It was school, homework and then badminton in that order. Outside of school, badminton, and family gatherings, I didn't have much of a social life. Dad's answer to keeping his kids on the right track was Sunday mass and getting them hooked on badminton, which he successfully did. This meant anything that could distract from us being the best we could with our studies and badminton (in that order) was out. I missed out on the teenage phase of parties, getting to know the opposite sex, smoking, drinking, and other rites of passage that most Australian teens go through.

Parties or social gatherings were uncomfortable events for me, particularly in the presence of strangers, especially girls. Growing up with three brothers and going to an all-boys school wouldn't have helped with that aspect of my life. I did have a sister, Clare, but she was 12 years older than I was. When I did occasionally go to a party, I'd disappear as soon as the lights went out and the disco ball came to life. I was terrified that one of my mates would drag me out to the dance floor to connect with some unsuspecting female, and I dreaded those awkward conversations due to my inferior small-talk skills.

When I turned 18, I packed my bags and departed for Sydney, Australia to pursue my final year of high school and complete the Higher School Certificate. My sole intent was to get to uni and get *that* degree.

The pressure of carrying the hopes of my parents and the guilt of having them give up so much to give my brothers and I the best chance of success, drove me to study hard. My cousin Xavier, with his wife Helen, very kindly and generously provided my best friend, Julian and

I with board and lodging during our first year in Australia. They would probably disagree with this viewpoint. Xavier frequently reminds my parents about how he actually never saw me study very much. My parents were frugal. They made sure I never had to worry about whether or not the next meal would be on the table. Apart from that and providing me with the tools I needed to succeed in badminton, we pretty much lived a no-frills life.

In my teenage years, I was often envious of and felt inferior to classmates who had newer, crisper school uniforms, pocket money to buy cassette tapes, vinyl records, transistors, and bikes, and were later even allowed to own a motorbike. If you wanted to be popular in school, these were the things you needed to have.

Arriving in Sydney, my strategy for dealing with the huge culture shock, homesickness, fending for myself for the first time in my life, and having to do all my school subjects in English (after 12 years of schooling where every subject had been in Malay) was to put my head down and work my tail off. I succeeded, became the dux of my school year and qualified to pursue a degree in Computer Science at the University of New South Wales (then regarded as one of the most prestigious universities in Australia). At uni, I fell in love with my first girlfriend and now wife and love of my life, Sue.

I completed my degree in the shortest possible time and was blessed to secure my first job shortly after as a Research Assistant at the University of New South Wales. I worked and studied full-time for two years, completing a Master of Commerce. My boss was the late Professor Cyril Brookes and I had the blessing of turning his life's work of helping organisations manage their knowledge from "proof-of-concept" into a commercialised software application that was marketed across Australia, the USA and Europe. By the good fortune of being his first employee, I progressed to VP of Product Development as the organisation grew.

In 1997, I moved my very young family (my kids Jeremy and Aaron were aged two and four) to Mountain View, California to start a new team in a collaborative venture with Netscape (the inventors of one of the first commercial web browsers). Working in the Silicon Valley in such a prestigious project would have been the dream of every IT profes-sional. In 1998, Professor Brookes decided to sell the company to Sun Microsystems, and I returned to Australia to join IBM (then one of the titans of the IT industry).

By 2001, I had risen to the position of Senior Manager and head of the Northern Region Software Services practice for IBM Australia. It was a tough year business-wise. 2000 had been exceptional – my team had helped build the Sydney Olympic Games results systems and website; something we all felt pretty good about. It had been very hard work, with an immovable deadline, but working on such a momentous project made it special for us.

That single project created so much work for my team that we had to call in consultants from all over the globe to help us. Whilst the hours were long, the result was worth it – the official Games' website handled unprecedented Internet traffic with 11.3 billion hits, a 1,700%

increase over the Nagano Games' official site in 1998. That year, my team exceeded our revenue targets easily! In hindsight though, whilst that appeared on the surface to be a great performance, the celebrations that followed masked the fact that without that project, we would have been quite a way off from hitting our mark.

By early 2001, the euphoria of the previous year's success ended with a thud when we received our new sales targets: "Grow the business by another 30%." You can only imagine how my sales colleagues would have felt. Not only did we have a 60% hole in our business, we were expected to grow it another 30%. This was in a year where the media was awash with how Sydney and Australia, in general, would suffer from the post-Olympics economic blues that had befallen its many predecessor host nations.

"There's no business out there." "Our clients are being incredibly conservative this year." "No one is keen to commit to large major IT infrastructure investments." "There goes my bonuses this year." Morale was plummeting within the business development team.

By the end of the first quarter, the writing was on the wall. We were way behind on our targets and I had too many consultants without billable projects. I pulled the team together and gave them my sobering assessment.

"Keep doing what we're doing and we'll keep getting what we're getting." I said, "The reality is that big organisations like IBM take on the opinions of independent third party research analysts such as International Data Corporation in defining their strategy and setting their targets. IDC is forecasting that in Australia, the software services business will grow by 30% in 2001. If IBM doesn't get its share, our competitors will. And that will significantly impact our future. If we truly believe that there's no business out there, I need you to help me manage my costs. Warming the bench and being a liability to our organisation isn't the answer. So if our international counterparts need help, please be prepared to take on an overseas assignment."

I could tell from their downcast looks that there certainly wasn't a lot of passion for that. Many had hoped life would be somewhat less hectic in 2001 after working many long hours and days for a few years leading up to the Olympics. Having to leave their families for an extended duration certainly didn't appeal to those who had planned to get their lives back to a semblance of normality, and I could tell they were feeling distinctly under-appreciated. But they seemed to see the sense in what I said and (though reluctant in some cases), they took on those overseas projects when they did come up.

By September that year, the ship was slowly but clearly turning around. My Country Manager was even complimentary of my efforts.

So, you can only imagine my shock and dismay when I received *that* call on that Friday. I responded to that bombshell with stunned silence. Totally caught off guard, the software engineer in me went into analysis mode: "What went wrong? What did *I* do wrong? Why didn't they consult me?"

And this went on for two … long … years.

During those two dark years, I struggled to get out of bed most mornings. While before I had prided myself in leading by example and being first in and last out, work now distinctly began to feel like a chore. I found myself often running late and feeling incredibly guilty about it. I meandered through the day, doing what I needed and what I was told, no more, no less. I simply struggled to find the drive to do more.

5 pm often seemed an eternity away, and I sometimes caught myself clock-watching. While I put on a brave front, I was hurting inside. I felt betrayed, and worse, felt like I'd betrayed my team. I felt like a fool thinking I had the power to protect and reward those who had performed. I'd get home feeling exhausted, look in the mirror and feel only guilt, knowing I had picked up a decent pay cheque that day but certainly not feeling like I had earned it.

My get-home routine during that period was to toss the keys on the kitchen counter and then slump into my couch, flicking through TV channels. Much of the time, I wasn't even watching and instead would analyse "What went wrong?" "What if I don't get one of those roles in the new structure?" "Why aren't they approaching me for that particular role?" I felt left out, resentful of peers who seemed to have the confidence of my superiors and frankly, angry that the organisation seemed to reward the "politically-savvy" employees. I felt hurt that they seemed to favour those with the "gift of the gab" rather than those who worked hard, did all that was asked of them but were just not so good at relationship building out of fear of being judged as apple polishers.

You can be great at what you do, have a decent intellect, have sought-after qualifications and even be drawing a decent pay cheque. But if you don't have the ability to bounce back from defeat, and stay optimistic, motivated, and confident during times of change, your ability to realise your highest potential and sense of happiness will be severely affected.

Fast forward to today - 15 years later. Today, I get to help organisations all over the world build high-performance culture and teams. My passion and work to help people realise their highest potential through their emotional and spiritual intelligence has reached more than 100 organisations in over 10 countries.

More than 20,000 people have attended our workshops and benefited from our coaching and training. Today, many call on my team and I to help resolve challenges such as low staff engagement levels, teams not working well together, people struggling from burnout, staying positive through change, and altogether transforming the hearts and minds of their teams to believe they can win.

The once shy, introverted, and socially-awkward nerd is now a confident and articulate public speaker and coach. Some even call me an inspirational speaker.

More importantly, some of the closest people in my life consider me to be the happiest person they know. I wake up each morning feeling blessed for the life I lead, the great relationships I have with my family, the decent physical shape I'm in and being able to do what I love doing best: making a difference to the people that matter the most to me.

My life turned around when I attended my first live personal development seminar, a Tony Robbins event called "Unleash the Power Within" in Sydney. This is where I first learned about emotional intelligence and mastery. To say the workshop was transformative would be an understatement. I learned that resilience, optimism and adaptability are in fact skills that can be learned. With the pace of unrelenting change that is occurring today and which is only going to grow exponentially, I believe such skills should be part of every school's curriculum.

That introduction into personal development was such an eye-opening and transformative experience for me. Since then, I've devoted much of the last 15 years to learning everything I can from many people considered to be luminaries in this wonderful industry. I've attended seminars, watched videos, and read and listened to books, tapes and podcasts from the likes of Dale Carnegie, Stephen R Covey, Howard Schultz, Jim Rohn, Denis Waitley, Brian Tracy, Dr John Demartini, Zig Ziglar, T Harv Eker, Joseph McClenddon III, Daniel Goleman, Jim Collins, Tim Ferriss, Robin Sharma and Andy Stanley amongst others.

Each breakthrough "ah-ha!" insight I learned would cause me to think: "Why aren't these principles, skills and strategies, which I consider essential life skills, compulsory teaching in schools and organisations?"

My experience in speaking, coaching, and training over the last decade has constantly reinforced how critical these skills are. Too many people are living in fear of their jobs, stressed about their futures and feeling helpless. Too many people suffer from Monday-itis and "thank God it's Friday" syndrome. Today, I have a career that I'm deeply passionate

WHAT'S GREAT ABOUT THIS?

about, that I feel blessed to have and one that gives me a deep sense of purpose and fulfilment.

For most of us, our career is one aspect that will consume the largest part of our living years. It also has the potential to meet all of our needs; our need to live, love, learn and to leave a legacy, at the highest level. I believe that life is way too short to *not* enjoy what we spend so much of our time on. New York bestselling author Simon Sinek, the genius behind one of the five most-watched TED talk videos of all time[1] – "How great leaders inspire action" and I share a simple vision – "a world where people wake up inspired to go to work".

And yet, I've learned that many people struggle and feel powerless in the face of change that affects every part of their life. Often, they end up living a life of quiet desperation. I know how that feels. And I have since learned that "the greatest tragedy in life is not death, but what we let die inside of us while we live" (a quote by Norman Cousins).

This is why I'm writing this book. To offer a message of hope and prac-tical tools and strategies for not just coping but thriving with change.

If you are:

- Experiencing high stress levels due to a great deal of uncertainty in your career or in your life in general.
- Worried and anxious about the future.

- Feeling down and somewhat helpless, perhaps even overwhelmed due to a recent setback.

- Lacking the energy, positivity and drive to move forward.

- Frozen in fear and doubt, and indecisive in the face of choices.

- Struggling to get out of bed.

- Having mood swings as a result of this and worried about the impact it is having in your personal life.

Or if you simply are looking for some inspiration, and perspectives that could give you an edge, and help you find and experience even greater fulfilment and success in your life, then there will be something in this book for you.

In this book, you will learn:

- How to turn any setback into an opportunity.

- How to read and transform any emotional state from one that disempowers you to one that makes you feel confident, optimistic, and inspired about the present and future.

- Simple, practical rituals you can build into your daily routine that will help you amp up your energy and passion.

- How to define what you'd ideally like to achieve in any situation you're in.

- How to feel a sense of control in times of uncertainty.

I write this with the fervent hope that you will benefit from my personal journey and the wisdom and learning I gained through my darkest years. Nothing you'll read in this book has been invented by me. I have just stood on the shoulders of giants and applied what I've interpreted to my life and situation.

I simply want to share with you what I've learned, hoping that you will benefit from my personal experience.

I want you to know that just like learning how to drive a car, solving a mathematical problem, or baking a cake, skills such as the ability to bounce back from defeat, stay positive through adversity, thrive through uncertainty and change, and experience fulfilment, can all be learned. I want you to learn about the deep and infinite well of resources that you already have and have total control over, how to bring them to life, and how to truly experience the joy and abundance you are destined for in this lifetime.

Most of all, I write this to offer you a dose of hope and inspiration, and an insight into the tremendous power that lies within you.

CHAPTER 1

Let's Get Started

You become what your subconscious habits dictate
Be outcome-oriented - begin everything you do
with the ideal end in mind
Decide in advance to be and achieve extraordinary outcomes
Make time to PAUSE and visualise ideal outcomes

"Begin with the end in mind."

– Stephen R Covey

I'm grateful that you've chosen to read this book and commend you for your decision. Out of countless books in the world, you've chosen this one, and I'm honoured and excited that you have. I truly believe there are no accidents in life, and there's a reason why you picked this book. Maybe the title caught your eye, or someone who cared about you suggested it. Maybe you received it as a gift.

But there's a reason you picked it up and are reading it now. Before we start, it's worthwhile reflecting for just a few moments on what those reasons are or could be.

What would you *love* to get out of a book like this? How could reading this enrich your life in some way?

I've dedicated a large chunk of the last 15 years of my life to learning what it takes to be both successful *and* fulfilled. Prior to that "wake up call" in 2001, I once thought that happiness was a by-product of success, and success a result of achievement. The higher the achievement, the more successful and happy I'd be. One of the key lessons I learned during those two dark years of self-doubt, anxiety, stress and fear, is that this is one of those greatest of fallacies in life. An "urban myth" I never challenged.

Back then I would have been considered - at least within my social circle and amongst those who were familiar with my background - to be a success, an achiever. Yet, I was far from fulfilled.

A wise man once taught me that we become who we are through the subconscious strategies (the habits of thought, emotions and behaviour) we run in our lives every waking moment of every day.

I recently watched a YouTube video[1] of a funny commercial showing a man and a woman, a few steps apart, riding up an escalator in an office building early in the morning. All of a sudden, the escalator stops with a "crash". It was interesting to observe the instinctive behaviour of the two people. After a couple of stunned seconds, the guy says "Oh. This is *not* good."

The lady mutters in exasperation. "I don't need this. I'm already late." The guy tries to calm her down saying "Somebody will come" and then yells out "Anybody out there??? Helloooo!!! We're stuck on an escalator and we ... need ... help." They both just stand there, frustrated. A third person would have just walked up the stairs! Same situation, different strategies driven by subconscious habit and clearly, one was more effective than the other.

And this is also true when it comes to reading books, dealing with change, adversity, failure, relationships or just pursuing success. Each of us has a different strategy for tackling this. Some jump right in, reading from cover to cover in one sitting. Others prefer to flip through chapters, picking titles they might find interesting.

Others start with a moment's reflection of the ideal outcomes they'd like to achieve through reading the book. Personally, I've found that those who start with the ideal end in mind will benefit the most from their investment of time.

I've written this book with you in mind, and what would help *you* stay most engaged to achieve the most optimal outcomes. With this out-come as my primary guide, I've chosen to write as if we were having a conversation. You'll find the book sprinkled with anecdotes. This is not an academic dissertation but is designed to be both an inspirational read and a practical how-to guide. Whenever I do share stories, mostly from my personal journey, I do this with the hope that you'll glean practical gems and inspiration that you can apply to get an even better outcome for yourself and others around you rise.

Because the best way of learning is through introspective reflection and active participation, the content includes activities that give you experiential learning, and Action Plans at the end of most chapters. This book also comes with an accompanying e-workbook that you can download for free from www.eqstrategist.com/f/whatsgreataboutthis.pdf. I encourage you to visit the site, download the workbook and enhance your reading by completing the recommended exercises.

Your active participation will deepen your understanding, retention, and subsequent application. It is through doing this that you will receive the most tremendous return on your biggest investment – your time.

In Stephen R Covey's bestseller titled "*7 Habits of Highly Effective People*", we learn that people who are highly effective, have habits that distinguish themselves from others. One of these key habits he calls "Begin with the End in Mind". People who are less than effective in life tend to be "task-oriented". They have a tendency to just jump right in. I used to be one of these people.

I've since learned that resilient, adaptable, effective, successful and fulfilled people (I'll refer to such people as "winners" from herein and those who are not as "whiners") are "outcome- oriented". They start everything they do by pausing and reflecting first on the outcomes they'd like to achieve from their actions.

How can you tell if someone is task or outcome oriented? By the habitual questions they ask in their heads in every situation. We subconsciously ask questions in our heads continually, and the answers to these questions affect how we feel, which drives our responses and the results we achieve. What questions pop up first thing every morning when you think about work? For me back then, it would invariably be: "What do I need to *do* today?" My life was filled with to-do lists. "I *need* to send the kids to school, then get to work. Run that meeting.

Finish that report. Fix that issue. Pick up the kids. Send them to music lessons."

I often felt overwhelmed. So much to do, so little time! I'd get home feeling exhausted, having ticked off most of the items and some others that somehow cropped up during the day. I'd lie on the couch, turn on the TV, doze off, wake up in the middle of the night, turn the telly off, creep into bed and the next morning, the alarm clock would ring and the routine would start all... Over ... again. Sounds familiar? I was on the treadmill called the "rat race", never questioning where I was headed and never passionate. I was just living on the expectation that as I long as I continued to climb the corporate ladder and make even more to sustain my family's ever growing needs, one day I'd somehow have enough to be able to "slow down" and finally do all the things I truly enjoyed.

When you study winners for as long as I have, you'll notice they all have similar strategies for dealing with work and life. And they're very different to what mine used to be. When I think of a winner, I think of someone like Sir Richard Branson, founder of the Virgin Group of companies. Someone most would regard as an uber-achiever and who seems to be having the time of his life. [2]Amongst his many business ventures, Branson formed Virgin Atlantic Airways in 1984, launched Virgin Mobile in 1999, and Virgin Blue in Australia (now named Virgin Australia) in 2000. He was ninth in the Sunday Times Rich List 2006 of the wealthiest people or families in the UK, worth slightly more than £3 billion.

He's not just successful in business, but also in life. In January 1991, Branson crossed the Pacific from Japan to Arctic Canada, 6,700 miles (10,800 km), in a balloon of 2,600,000 cubic feet (74,000 m^3). This broke the record, with a speed of 245 miles per hour (394 km/h). In March 2004, Branson set a record by travelling from Dover to Calais in a Gibbs Aquada in one hour, 40 minutes and six seconds, the fastest crossing of the English Channel in an amphibious vehicle.

I've personally met and trained staff who've worked for Branson and they invariably speak in admiration of a man well-loved with an incredibly down-to-earth personality. He has a tendency to show up in a staff canteen in jeans and a shirt, eating a sandwich he's brought from home, and meeting and connecting with his people.

Not bad for a bloke with dyslexia who dropped out of school at 16, with no tertiary qualifications.

Each time I visit my parents in Malaysia (dad is 80 this year and mum almost 78), I'd often ask them "How's life?" Invariably, they'll say, "It's going great!" They'd speak with passion about their recent trip to Jogjakarta where they were able to visit the Borobudur, meet beautiful people and sample great local fare at reasonable prices. Then they'd tell me about their next planned trip to Chiang Mai, Thailand with a group of friends.

I'd often wonder how they could afford to do this with the modest pension they have. In recognition for having served in public office as a teacher for most of their adult life, both dad and mum receive a humble pension of approximately RM$1,000 a month. This translates to roughly AUD$350. The answer? Two words: Air Asia. Low cost airlines have made it possible for so many to experience so much of the world and certainly in the case of my parents and other retirees on a modest pension, made their retirement so much more interesting.

Tony Fernandes, the wonderful entrepreneur who founded Air Asia counts Branson as one of his mentors[3]. Branson founded Virgin Atlantic Airways, a low-cost airline, in 1984, during a period where the conventional wisdom was that the commercial aviation industry was so competitive that even full-cost airlines struggled to make a profit. Branson wrote in his autobiography[4] of the decision to start an airline:

'My interest in life comes from setting myself huge, apparently unachievable challenges and trying to rise above them...from the perspective of wanting to live life to the full, I felt that I had to attempt it.'

His vision and that of Tony Fernandes were similar – 'Now everyone can fly'.

Another person I consider a "winner" is the late Steve Irwin, Australia's "Crocodile Hunter". He lived more lifetimes in his relatively short 44 years on this earth than others who might have twice his lifespan. Whenever I travel in Asia and I'm asked where I'm from, I say "Australia" and often I get "Crikey!" (one of Steve's favourite catch phrases) in response. He is probably Australia's greatest ambassador in Asia, with the "Crocodile Hunter" TV program being a favourite amongst so many. This is a man who has done more than most to elevate the general consciousness about the need to conserve nature for our future generations. To me, he epitomised someone who lived life to the fullest, living each and every day as if it were his last.

In a tribute to her husband, "My Steve"[5], Terri Irwin writes about her memory of her last time with Steve. The family had just completed a croc research trip together in outback Australia. A small plane had come to take her and her kids home. Steve and his crew would take another flight to what would turn out to be his last expedition and his encounter with the stingray that would end his life. As the plane took off, Terri and her daughter Bindi looked back and saw Steve, on top of his ute, as animated as ever waving a warm and fond farewell to the family he loved so much.

When you study folks like Branson and Irwin, you will find that they are what I call **outcome-oriented** people. The first question that pops into their head every morning tends to be along the lines of *"what will make today extraordinary?"* This habit of starting every journey with the ideal end in mind transcends everything they do – they apply it to every meeting, vacation and project they undertake.

So, using the words of the late Steve Jobs, "We don't get a chance to do that many things, and every one should be really excellent. Because this is our life. Life is brief, and then you die, you know? And we've all chosen to do this with our lives. So it better be damn good. It better be worth it."

Think about it. Take two people - one who wakes up each and every morning asking, "What do I need to *do* today?" and another who asks "what will make it *extraordinary*?" Do you think these would be very different people with very different experiences of life? Who do you think would be more effective and fulfilled?

Action Plan

Let's put this habit into practise. Set a goal now for how you'd like to feel as a result of reading this book. What would make you feel that way? What are three to five outcomes you'd love to achieve - things you'd like to experience or learn that would make the time you've chosen to invest in reading this, well worth it? If you have downloaded and printed the workbook, go ahead and write your answers in that workbook. Otherwise, just write this down in a journal somewhere.

Have you written down some goals that you're truly excited about? Imagine you've finished reading the book AND it has helped you achieve the outcomes above. How would that make you feel?

What I've learned about winners is that whatever they decide to do, they decide first and foremost to achieve an extraordinary outcome. They have the habit of pressing the PAUSE button to reflect, to use their imagination and to visualise IDEAL outcomes before deciding on what and how to do what they do.

Now that you're clear about your outcomes, decide to get the most from this book by taking notes, participating in the exercises and taking action to apply what you've learned. Let's jump right in and get started.

CHAPTER 2

Disruption and Change - the New Norm

Change is happening and it's happening faster than ever

Embrace change and adapt or risk being obsolete

Disruption and change present both opportunities and threats

It's not the change, it's how you respond that determines your destiny

Don't let change happen to you, let it happen for you

The first step to being resilient is to accept the change

Instead of asking the "Blame Why", learn to focus on the "Curious Why"

"We must free ourselves of the hope that the sea will ever rest. We must learn to sail the high winds."

— Aristotle Onassis

Change or Be Changed

In the popular 2008 YouTube video presentation titled *"Did you know 3.0 Shift Happens"*[1] created, researched, and designed by Sony/BMG, Karl Fisch, Scott McLeod and Jeff Brenman, the following messages are streamed through a thumping soundtrack:

- If you're one in a million in China, there are 1,300 people just like you.

- China will soon become the number 1 English speaking country in the world.

- The 25% of India's population with the highest IQ is greater than the total population of the United States.

- India has more honours kids than America has kids.

- The top 10 in-demand jobs in 2010 didn't exist in 2004.

- We're currently preparing students for jobs that don't yet exist, using technologies that haven't been invented, in order to solve problems we don't even know are problems yet.

- The US Department of Labor estimates that today's learner will have 10-14 jobs by the age of 38.

- One in four workers has been with the current employer for less than a year.

- One in two has been there less than five years.

The underlying message is clear – *"change is happening and it's happening faster than ever"*. "Disruption" is the buzzword of the day. [2]Harvard Business School professor and disruption guru Clayton Christensen says that a disruption displaces an existing market, industry, or technology and produces something new and more efficient and worthwhile. It is at once destructive and creative. Everywhere I go today, nations and organisations are pressured to turn around old-school "do-as-you're-told", process-oriented cultures to one where everyone, from the CEO to the janitor are expected and given time to innovate. After all, one great idea, well executed, could turn their organisation into the next Apple, Uber, Amazon or Tesla. These ideas catalysed tectonic paradigm shifts that overnight spawned massive opportunities for enterprising upstarts, and wrought destructive change to former industry titans slow to adapt (think Eastman Kodak, Yahoo!, Sony and Sun Microsystems).

Take the example of Kickstarter, founded in 2009 by Perry Chen, Yancey Strickler and Charles Adler and based out of Brooklyn, New York. Kickstarter is a crowdfunding platform that has helped finance thousands of projects from video games to urban farms. It's a super efficient way for creative people to raise money – from the masses. The potential impact this innovation can have on markets is mind-bending. Consider what it can do to the film industry. In 2013, "Inocente" became the first Kickstarter-funded film[3] (it raised $52,527 on the crowdfunding site) to win an Oscar project Academy.

The axiom "change or be changed" is more profound than it has ever been. Yesterday's disrupters are being disrupted today! Take for ex-ample the wonderful phenomenon that's Uber, the ride-hailing inno-vator from San Francisco. Today, thanks to Uber and Uber clones (the idea has spawned numerous competitors across the globe), one can be self-employed or start a business (part or full-time) overnight with zero to miniscule capital, business experience and skills. Equipped simply with a driver's license, ownership of a vehicle with a decent mainte-nance history and a smartphone with a data plan, one can start creating and getting paid for their service, delivering everything from people, food and parcels. Since its beginnings in 2008, Uber has taken the world by storm not just economically, but also politically, socially and in some cases "literally". [4]In cities from Kuala Lumpur to Jakarta to Paris, there have been numerous reported incidents of noisy and even violent protests by mobs of taxi drivers, angered by a significant drop in earnings when Uber was launched.

Whilst this is presenting a significant threat to the livelihood of cab-bies, it also represents a massive opportunity for job creation. The con-cept has extended beyond taxi, bus and limo hailing to enabling people to literally have anything – food, documents, goldfish, and even mas-seurs delivered to their doors through the help of private motorcycle or bicycle couriers. Think of the massive impact this innovation has and will continue to have on traditional taxi companies and the entire transportation industry.

This phenomenon has (for the most part) been warmly embraced by consumers worldwide. As a frequent traveller who is both time-poor and frankly, could do with friendlier cabbies and better-smelling cabs – I'm an unabashed fan. And so when I visited Shanghai in March 2016, I was amazed to learn how a Chinese version of Uber called Didi Chuxing, had been beating Uber at its own game. Didi Chuxing was formed by the merger of two Chinese rivals, Didi Dache and Kuaidi Dache, who were backed respectively by China's two largest internet companies - Tencent (owner of Wechat, China's largest social media platform) and Alibaba (China's largest online retailer).

By the first quarter of 2016, Didi Chuxing had gained 85% of the ride-hailing business in China, compared to Uber with 8%. In the battle for market supremacy, both organisations, awash with multi-billion dollar venture capital funding, had invested tens of millions of dollars in incentives for both drivers and riders. Uber's chief executive, Travis Kalanick, famously said the company had been losing USD$1 billion annually trying to grab market share[5]. On 1 August 2016, Uber decided that enough was enough and took the "if you can't beat 'em, join 'em" approach, selling its China business to Didi Chuxing for a 20% share of the combined business.

In the first quarter of 2015, when Uber was relatively new to China, it had a market valuation of approximately USD$40 billion versus Didi Chuxing's valuation of USD$8.75 billion at the time of the Didi Kuadi merger. So, how did Didi Chuxing win what many would have regarded as a battle between David versus Goliath? Didi had modelled its business on many of the things that consumers, like me, love so much about Uber – the convenience of being able to order a ride at the touch of a button, to know precisely where the driver was and when it would arrive, the security (for both driver and rider) of not having to carry cash on-board, and the peace of mind of not worrying about whether or not you were going to be taken for a ride (excuse the pun) by a cabbie because you could choose for the route taken to be the one defined by the GPS. While its success has been attributed to numerous factors including the typical "They had a better understanding of the Chinese way of doing business", Didi Chuxing had one key differentiator that I personally believe made all the difference. It was able to capitalise on another significant disruption (in the finance sector) that's taking the world by storm, and certainly in China - the move towards paying for purchases through a mobile payment app on your smartphone.

Nowadays if you live in a city area in China, as long as you have a smart phone, you can pay for almost anything with your phone, either through Tencent's Wechat Wallet or Alibaba's Mobile Alipay. This includes purchases you make at supermarkets, local convenient stores, restaurants, hotels, movies, transportation, and even some street food stands. In 2012, Wechat's extraordinary success as a social media platform led many Chinese IT companies to shift their focus to the mobile app market. With the Chinese government encouraging mobile payment development, all was set for Tencent and Alibaba's mobile payment apps to be the "next big thing". The key hurdle they had to overcome was a cultural one – the Chinese are mostly quite cautious when paying, and most aren't exactly fans of novelty gadgets. But they do love one thing more - discounts or kickbacks! The cab-calling apps Didi and Kuaidi became the perfect user traffic introducers. You could use Didi to call a cab and pay 30 yuan in cash, but if you paid the cabbie by Tencent Wallet (redirected from Didi), you only had to pay 10. Do you think the typical Chinese consumer would be willing to save 20 yuan - 3 or 4 US dollars – simply by using an already built-in feature in another app through just a few taps? You bet!! And now they were hooked-up with Wechat Wallet. That's what Tencent really wanted.

Tencent and Alibaba invested an extraordinary amount of money to pay for all the unbelievable kickbacks. Extraordinary for a cab-calling app, but totally reasonable if you wanted to mark your territory in the biggest market in the world, which is the most advanced in mobile payments. With Uber China (before it was bought out by Didi Chuxing), you had a cool personal "valet" in your pocket that could help you get a decent car whenever you wanted to go somewhere. With Didi and through its tight integration with Wechat Wallet, you had a personal "valet" on steroids who could help you not just hail a ride but also book tickets, pay for meals, check electric bills, etc.

In China, Uber the disrupter had became the disrupted through the innovation of another visionary who picked up on their idea, made small but significant improvements to it, and through bold and rapid execution, created a business that went from being an unknown six years ago, to an organisation valued at US$28 billion as of June 2016.

What does that tell you about the essential skills we need to not just survive, but ideally thrive during these times of disruption and change? Resilience. Adaptability. Resourcefulness. Creativity. Innovation. The skills to stay positive, confident, optimistic and motivated, no matter what.

And if you're a manager, the ability to lead change and help with your team's adaptability and resilience and create an innovative culture.

And yet I wish I could recall going through a subject called "change 101" in school, or uni. With 13 years at school and five in uni, completing both undergraduate and master's degrees, and there wasn't a single topic on resilience or dealing with change. What does that tell you about our education system?

It's not personal

Everywhere I go, I see evidence of transformational change. In 2016 alone, the Brexit and Trump votes were startling examples of unanticipated changes that have started and will have a far-reaching and profound political, social and economic impact globally. The genius of human innovation afforded by game-changing technologies such as the internet, Wi-Fi, virtual reality and the resulting effects of globalisation and the growing middle-class and wealth of third world economies are creating a rise of "sunset" industries and putting a huge strain on jobs.

Australia has just been through a mining boom, spurred by the seemingly insatiable demand for its resources from the growth story of the millennium - China! But now Australia's dependence has meant that as the Chinese economy has slowed, as a result of building too quickly then needing time to allow consumers to buy and use what's already been developed, the mining sector is going through post-boom blues. The lack of foresight in planning and preparing for this change means that Australia and its people are going through a period of pain.

Downsizing and restructuring is the norm. Mine closures have caused the loss of thousands of jobs with massive flow-on effects in related sectors – real estate, tourism, oil and gas, staff recruitment, mining equipment, hospitality, service industries, and transportation are all affected. The government coffers are significantly in deficit, which means managers are pressured to find cost savings everywhere. A drive towards improving productivity is the buzzword, with many departments at both the federal and state levels amalgamating to eke out efficiencies.

Whenever I travel to Singapore, I love looking out the window as the plane descends on this amazing metropolis. It never ceases to amaze me seeing scores of ships with massive cargo containers parked off the coast of this port with its strategic location. I imagine a "toll gate" out there off the coast and the "ka-ching" sound of a till as each ship stops to refuel or settle in to replenish its supplies.

Ten years from now, however, this picture could be very different. The ice caps in the North Pole have been melting for years now - an effect of global warming. The Singaporean government knows this and is visionary enough to realise that before long, ships from Northern Asia and Europe might prefer a more direct, cost effective route through the north, unencumbered by treacherous icebergs. On 30 April 2016, the Straits Times of Singapore published an article titled "The Thai Canal that will Change Singapore Forever". It spoke about Thailand building a canal through the land chokepoint called the Isthmus of Kra with financial aid from China. If built, the canal would link the Indian Ocean and the South China Sea directly, bypassing Singapore. This link, first mooted in the 17th century by French developer Ferdinand de Lesseps, would shorten voyages from Europe to China by 1,200 km and end Singapore's status as a top sea hub. This will present a significant challenge to its business landscape. The country has been restructuring its economy over the past five years, with a focus on raising productivity in order to drive quality growth.

Flattening playing fields and globalisation have enabled third world economies to thrive and their success is now posing huge challenges to more established economies like the US, England, Japan, Singapore, and Australia, where labour costs are significantly higher. Higher costs of production have driven companies to move their manufacturing plants abroad to countries like China, Vietnam, Thailand, Indonesia, Malaysia or outsourcing to the Philippines or India which have an abundance of skilled labour at much cheaper rates.

Professionals in developed nations who reach their 40s or 50s are confronted with the real prospects of redundancies and having to put up with diminishing lifestyles. Singapore and Australia are possibly the nations with the most highly qualified taxi drivers in the world – former engineers, IT professionals, bankers, and accountants who have lost their jobs are resorting to driving cabs and working for Uber to make a living.

Since 2013, I have been travelling to the United Arab Emirates two to three times a year to run leadership courses. Before oil was discovered in the 1950s the UAE's economy was dependent on fishing and a declining pearl industry. But since oil exports began in 1962, the country's society and economy have been transformed. Over the last two years, the oil industry, with its history of booms and busts, has been in its deepest downturn since the 1990s, if not earlier. Over the last five years, the nation has been through a significant transformation as it restructures its economy to one that's significantly more diversified.

On 8 September 2016, Reuters reported that the Saudi Arabian government had ended talks aimed at saving construction giant Saudi Oger, which was facing a multi-billion-dollar debt restructuring to stave off collapse. Oger is one of two mega-contractors charged with implementing the grand infrastructure and development plans of the kingdom, building everything from defence installations to schools and hospitals. The fall in oil prices since mid-2014 and the resulting sharp state spending cuts, had weighed heavily on Oger's business, given its size and reliance on government contracts. The impact on Oger's staff and other stakeholders had been significant, with Oger struggling to meet its financial obligations. In this downturn, scores of companies have gone bankrupt and an estimated 250,000 oil workers have lost their jobs.

As I travel around the world, I'm constantly amazed at the pace at which disruptive technologies are transforming industries overnight. Online e-commerce has transformed the way we buy things, and retail companies with traditional brick-and-mortar businesses have had to revamp their business models or risk being made obsolete by smaller, nimbler, tech-savvy retailers who are able to pass on significant cost savings to consumers due to their lower overheads. The ride-sharing company Uber is a case in point, with its revolutionary business model challenging traditional taxi companies and their staff all around the world.

By 2020, driverless cars will be pretty standard fare, posing incredible challenges to employment - not just in Australia but around the globe. A cabbie in Singapore told me just the other day that the country has been trialling a driverless taxi for the past year. As a nation whose economy revolves around a $200 billion transport and logistics industry[13], Australia waving goodbye to its truck drivers will have far-reaching effects. After a futuristic fleet of self-driving "smart trucks" drove across Europe from Sweden to the Netherlands in May 2016, TechCrunch predicted, "no technology will automate away more jobs — or drive more economic efficiency[13]". With robot drivers who don't need to eat or sleep, our trucks will be carrying goods at breakneck speeds within decades. The impact on jobs will be significant. Businesses linked with truck drivers and the roadside will struggle or be forced to close as well, from service stations, to cafes, to motels.

In Australia, there's a common saying: "There are only three things that are certain in life – death, taxes, and *change.*" So if you're going through change, know that you're not alone. This is a worldwide phenomenon that's unlikely to slow down in the years to come. Everywhere I go, even if an organisation is doing well, the team is undergoing change and being challenged to meet extraordinary growth targets to fulfil stakeholder expectations. If an organisation is not doing too well, it's being challenged to restructure in order to stay relevant.

Don't take it personally. Change has, and will always be constant. And it's not likely to slow down anytime soon. Your organisation needs to continually change and reinvent itself to stay relevant and where possible, stay ahead of the curve.

Heed the words of Jim Rohn, one of my favourite philosophers and teachers: "It's not the blowing of the wind that determines your destination. It's the set of your sail." By applying the thinking and strategies in this book, you'll not only be able to survive, but thrive on these changes.

Our human need to grow drives change

> *"If you're standing still, you're moving backwards."*
>
> — *Wayne Bennett, famous NRL coach in Australia*

> *"It is not the strongest of the species that survives, nor the most intelligent that survives. It is the one that is most adaptable to change."*
>
> — *Charles Darwin*

There are many factors affecting our economy, which in turn is putting enormous strain on our workplaces either in positive or negative ways. Many of these are economic, brought about by technological advancements and growing economies. Some of these are social, such as ageing populations, and the growing disparity between the haves and have-nots in developing and developed economies. Some of these are environmental, like the effects of global warming. And some of these may be political, such as the doctrines of a political party, or even the politics within an organisation itself, where the clamour for position, power or control can drive decisions that affect us.

Many of these changes are driven by a fundamentally basic human need – to **grow**. As a living organism, humans are ultimately designed to grow. Not just in one's lifetime, but taking a multi-generational view into perspective, each generation seeks to be even better than its predecessor. The pursuit of growth, or fulfilment – "to realise our highest potential," is a fundamental need programed into our DNA.

In Dan Pink's book, *Drive: The Surprising Truth About What Motivates Us*, he talks about the three intrinsic motivators that drive human behaviour – the quest for Mastery, Autonomy and Purpose. Humans innately seek to solve the world's problems, firstly just because they're there to be solved (mastery) and because we're purpose driven engines, we want to solve and make things better for our loved ones and others around us (purpose). We're also born to be "free" and invention or creation is a powerful way of satisfying this inner drive for freedom (autonomy).

In Pink's book, he tells the story of an experiment to study primate behaviour conducted in the 1940s by Harry F. Harlow, a professor of psychology at the University of Wisconsin. Harlow and two colleagues gathered eight rhesus monkeys for a two-week experiment on learning. The researchers devised a simple mechanical puzzle. Solving it required three steps: pull out the vertical pin, undo the hook, and lift the hinged cover. Pretty easy for humans and supposedly far more challenging for a 13-pound lab monkey.

The experimenters placed the puzzles in the monkeys' cages to observe how they reacted. Almost immediately, something strange happened. Unbidden by any outside urging and unprompted by the experimenters, the monkeys began playing with the puzzles with focus, determination, and what looked like enjoyment. And in short order, they began figuring out how the contraptions worked. The experimenters found this a bit odd since nobody had taught the monkeys how to remove the pin, slide the hook, and open the cover, and nobody had rewarded them with food, affection, or even quiet applause when they succeeded. Harlow concluded that the performance of the task itself provided intrinsic reward. The monkeys solved the puzzles simply because they found it gratifying to solve puzzles. They enjoyed it. **The joy of the task was its own reward.**

And so it is with humans. When I visited with a dear friend in Newcastle last year, I was amused to see both her and her partner slumped on a couch, exhausted by their attempts to meet the ongoing demands of an energetic 18-month old. Jack was intensely focussed on picking the lock on the cabinet that housed the family TV. They couldn't keep him still. Like the energizer bunny that keeps on going, Jack just enjoyed working out the different combination numbers his parents kept setting on the lock to prevent him from getting to the electronics.

It's not going to go away

Many of the changes we're going through in the workplace are a result of economic change that's unprecedented, both in terms of scale and pace. Our economy (which includes how goods are produced, exchanged, distributed and consumed) is an important aspect of society and as the economy has evolved over time, societies have, too.

Prior to the 18th century, humans largely lived off the land or sea and we made our own houses and clothes. The agricultural revolution (a period between the 18th century and end of the 19th century) initiated the beginning of the evolution of economy. During the agricultural revolution, man's quest for growth and improvement resulted in inventions like the plough, the wheel, and a number system that allowed us to perform tasks more efficiently. These changes had both positive and negative effects on society. More practical and efficient farming practices like rotating crops and using fertilizer led to better and bigger surpluses of food. During this age, towns and cities grew and particular regions became centres for trade and commerce.

However, as with every change, during this period we also saw some negative impacts, including a greater division of labour and status in which the wealthy gained control of surplus resources and power became more centralised. The wealthy were therefore able to afford a better quality of living, and differences in social classes by ethnicity and gender increased.

Work that was previously done by individuals was now being performed in centralised settings in cities with large factories and on equipment capable of producing massive amounts of products quickly. The industrial revolution also led to negative factors, such as overcrowding in cities due to the large migration of people from urban settings to be closer to factories. Skilled workers were replaced by low-skilled workers who left agricultural work.

The post-industrial society (also sometimes known as the information society or the knowledge revolution) is a more recent development. While previous revolutions were established on the production of goods, the knowledge revolution has seen a shift from products to ideas and knowledge, from hands-on skills to literacy skills and the decentralisation of the workforce because work is not centralised around city factories. In the many developed countries around the globe today, as much as half of the workforce is currently employed in the service industries, including government, sales, banking and education.

Each revolution was a seismic change to our lives, creating a great deal of uncertainty. Within the knowledge age itself, we've seen numerous phases of change, each with progressively shorter timeframes. In my parents' generation, it was very common for someone to enter the workforce knowing that they might have one job for life. My parents were certainly teachers from their first to final day of formal employment! Today, the US labour department predicts that by the age of 38, most people will have had between 10-14 jobs. Not only are frequent job changes the norm, but it has even been predicted that a person starting out in the workforce today may have up to seven career changes before his or her working life is up.

Technology and innovation will continue to drive change

The invention of computers, followed by the Internet and then Wi-Fi, has made the world considerably smaller. Travel is cheaper than it has ever been and dramatic improvements have permeated every part of our lives. Entire industries have become obsolete with shorter and shorter cycles. Horses to cars. Beta tapes to CDs. CDs to MP3s. Many "giants" of their respective industries have been left on the wayside and gone bust with each paradigm shift. Digital Equipment Corporation, Honeywell, Wang Computers, Blackberry, MySpace - all giants in their respective industries at one time are literally either gone or have become largely irrelevant.

My life today gives me infinitely more options and "power" than the richest man in the world had 50 years ago. I have more power in my phone and smartwatch than the machine that took the first man to the moon[17]! I can watch the same TV program with my family who may be in three different time zones, chatting live with them and experiencing what they're experiencing through an LCD panel and Skype — often free of charge.

The first step to dealing with change is acceptance. To accept that change is NOT going to slow down anytime soon. And usually there's nothing we can do to stop it. We may and should feel uneasy about impending change (it keeps us sharp, alert and on edge, which is essential to feel truly alive), however, to remain optimistic that every change may bring about peril but will also bring about significant opportunity.

Al Gore, who first so powerfully and effectively alerted the world to the changes that would be brought about by climate change, highlights six key areas that will drive global change in the years to come in his book "The Future: Six Drivers of Global Change"[18]. These include ever-increasing economic globalisation, digital communications, the shifting balance of global political, economic and military power, a deeply flawed economic compass, genomic, biotechnology, neuroscience and life sciences revolutions, and the radical disruption of the relationship between human beings and the earth's ecosystem. He also writes, "There is no prior period of change that remotely resembles what humanity is about to experience. We have gone through revolutionary periods of change before, but none as powerful or as pregnant with the fraternal twins — peril and opportunity — as the ones that are beginning to unfold."

Accepting that change is here to stay, and that *how* you respond is what truly matters, is what this book is all about. This book will give you practical skills, tools and techniques for not only coping with, but thriving on change. Instead of dwelling on the question, "Why is this happening to me?" you'll learn how to focus instead on "How can I take advantage of the opportunities presented in any situation?"

Accept that change is here to stay

I realise now, that during those two years when I struggled with the blowing of the wind, it wasn't the change but my habitual, subconscious strategies that I was using that made that time such a struggle.

I took the change personally. My habitual instinct was to analyse and to keep asking what I call the "Blame Why". "Why are they doing this to *me*?" "Why is this happening to *me*?" The answers that my mind dredged up only made me feel depressed — "People don't care. You were misguided to think you were important. The new Director is making changes only to show that he's doing something new." This strategy for dealing with change is not unlike the ones shown by the couple moving up the escalator. It's what I call the "Freeze and Blame" strategy. It's a strategy that gets us nowhere and is only a pathway to frustration. With prolonged and sustained use, it can lead down a path to powerlessness, loss of confidence, and even depression.

When I learned not to focus on the winds of change, which I had no control over, but on the setting of the sail, which I had total control over, my first step was to **assume that there were really good and compelling reasons for the change.**

I decided first and foremost to take my emotional self and other people out of the equation and instead research the underlying factors driving the change. Instead of asking the "Blame Why" and living in victim-ville and denial, I decided to ask the "Curious Why" with intent to take the positive learnings from the situation.

When I decided to be open-minded by asking some of my senior colleagues what had actually led to this change, I learned that for several years, our department had been struggling to stay relevant. Whilst our "revenues" were seemingly increasing, our margins were being stretched by two major trends buffeting our business at the time.

The first trend was that the price of software licensing was significantly declining each year. The introduction of the Internet, rising competition, and the growing prevalence of software piracy meant that our customers were moving towards software providers who were the most cost-competitive. While in the past, releasing new versions of market-leading technology with more features and functions meant being able to charge more per license, this trend was reversing. Today, consumers can have free access to sophisticated, powerful software that has cost its makers millions of dollars in investment. In the 1990s, this was unheard of! I couldn't have imagined any software entrepreneur being willing to take all that risk and invest a significant chunk of his or her personal fortune and time into building an organisation that would give away its intellectual property.

At the same time, our business costs were rising. Staff who were gaining in experience expected salary increments. The cost of office space and utilities were soaring as Sydney became a sought-after destination after the additional fame gained through a highly successful Olympics. This meant that for several years now, in actual terms, we hadn't been profitable as a business unit. The situation was clearly unsustainable.

With more research, I also learned that **such change, like every other, brings about both downsides and upsides**. From the angle of opportunity, the rise of the Internet meant that the market was both fearful of being left behind, and hungry to capitalise on its massive potential. A common boardroom discussion across the globe at the time would have been about how they could create an online presence and business as quickly as possible, and with minimum risk. My team was well positioned to capitalise on this. We had the total package – hardware, software, and skills – but needed to first stem the "bleeding" as soon as possible and then restructure to turn ourselves from a product-oriented organisation (with brands like Lotus, WebSphere, etc.) into one that was solution oriented (e-commerce portals, knowledge management, collaboration solutions).

My realisation that my leaders were actually taking difficult, courageous, but inspired steps to create an even better future for my organisation was the first step towards my recovery and my journey towards creating a different and better future for me, my family, and my organisation. I also learned that my habits of being a head down, bum up doer had meant I wasn't putting enough focus and time on truly leading my team, scouring the environment for dangers, threats and opportunities, and constantly resetting the direction and path it needed to take.

I started to feel much more empowered and determined to focus on what I had control over (how I could set the sail to take advantage of the opportunities presented) rather than what I had no control over (trends and the decision by my superiors to make the change).

> *"God, grant me the serenity to accept the things I cannot change, Courage to change the things I can, and wisdom to know the difference."*
>
> — *The Serenity Prayer, Reinhold Niebuhr*

Action Steps

1. For a change that you're going through right now in the workplace, reflect on what may be the underlying reasons for the change. Assuming that your leaders are making great decisions about the change, why is the status quo so unsustainable that the change has to be made?

2. Assuming the change has been successfully implemented, how might that have a positive impact on your organisation, your team, your customers and your staff?

3. If you're still uncertain about the reasons for the change, do some research. Be proactive in seeking out any documentation or available information on the background of the drivers of the change. Speak to someone who's more intimately involved with the change – this could be your manager, one of your peers, another manager who's leading the change, or an HR manager. Seek them out to have an informal conversation. Let them know that you're curious about the change and would like to learn more. During the meeting, ask questions like "What are the factors leading to the need for change? What does a successful change

look like? Who will that benefit? In what way?"

Choose your battles

I've had workshop participants ask me, "What if I've done all the research and come to the conclusion that the change is not the right thing, it's politically motivated, and I just can't agree with it?"

My advice to them is reflect on the options they have:

Option 1 – do nothing but complain, choose to be a victim.

Result: You'll probably struggle with the change, not have a great time, and feel a fair bit of stress. Your struggle is not going to be lost on others and this will probably affect their confidence in you and your career prospects - making life even harder for you in your organisation. Not a great result for your self-esteem.

Option 2 – learn and apply the skills of effective influence and do your best to influence constructively, optimistically, and with great diplomacy.

Result: You may achieve a great outcome and influence a change for the better. Even if you're unsuccessful, your skills will grow, your leadership traits won't be lost on others, and you'll strengthen invaluable life skills.

Option 3 – you decide that things are way too advanced, there are too many forces outside your control, and that in spite of your best intentions, your level of rapport with your superiors is not deep enough that you'll create a positive impact.

A lot of energy and effort will be expanded for something that will likely come to nought. You choose to pick your battles wisely and decide instead to focus on what you have total control over, putting your energies on what you CAN do to make the most positive difference to your customers and staff.

Result: You grow in skills and confidence. Your positive attitude will likely rub off on others and may not be lost on your superiors. Your actions will deepen the trust they have in you which means you'll have greater opportunities to influence decisions in the future. You continue to enjoy what you do because it is meaningful.

Option 4 – you decide that the change is so much against your personal values that you simply cannot put up with the new situation. You decide to be proactive and find another opportunity where you can excel, being careful not to burn your bridges.

Result: Your self-esteem stays intact. This could well open up the door to significant new opportunities and adventures for you.

Several years ago, I caught up with a dear friend who tried Option 2 and then went for Option 3. Virginia was a Senior Manager for a major federal government agency. We had met through a conference on Change and Resilience where both of us had been on the speaking panel. I caught up with her one evening and over dinner I casually asked her what her thoughts were on a new government initiative that was hitting the airwaves and attracting a lot of controversy. She said quite frankly, she felt her department was rushing through a particular policy for political reasons and that much more could be done before they pushed out what she felt was "half-cooked".

Knowing that she was a person of great principles, I asked her how she was able to stay so positive in a situation where she didn't agree with her superiors. She said "Dom, in life I have learned that you have to pick your battles. I knew changing the decision that had already been made would have been very difficult but I could reconcile myself by focussing on all the things I had total control over."

Virginia continued. "Let me give you an example," she said, "one of the challenges in Australia is getting trained doctors out to regional areas. Last week, I learned of a doctor who had applied to migrate to Australia, had met all our conditions and was prepared to take up an assignment in one of our remote regions. His application had however become stuck in a stack of papers with managers either procrastinating or not being willing to make a decision to endorse it. Finally after a few phone calls I was able to get the file, make a decision, explain to my superiors why I made the decision and know that a few weeks from now, I would have contributed to the well-being of that community who now have access to the better healthcare they've been crying out for and that they deserve."

I was so impressed with her mind-set – focussing on all the things she had control over and being determined to make a difference even in a situation where there were things that were imperfect.

CHAPTER 3

How your EQ affects your Resilience

*The hardest part about dealing with change is
dealing with fear and uncertainty*

Your emotions affect your actions and your outcomes

Your resilience is largely a factor of your EQ

Being resilient starts with being self-aware

*Some emotions empower and others disempower
us in times of change*

Choose how you wish to feel and cultivate Power Emotional Tools

"*The only thing to fear is fear itself.*"

- Roosevelt

The E-A-R Model of How We Process Change

We know that change is a constant and it's happening faster than ever. If your organisation is not radically reinventing itself and in double-quick time in the face of economic changes or competitors offering disruptive technologies or models of doing business, it's quite possible that it will be irrelevant overnight.

Let's take a look at some of the biggest layoffs in American history[1]:

- In 2015, Conoco Philips announced a plan to cut 10% of workforce due to the downturn in oil prices.

- In 1993, Sears laid off 50,000 employees due to an unwillingness to compete with Walmart which had aggressively undercut it at every turn.

- In 1993, IBM laid off 60,000 employees - the largest in American history - as the mainframe computing giant was slow to adapt to the disruption posed by the uptake of personal computers and other technologies.

- 2012 saw the demise of Kodak, which had been slow to reinvent its' film-based business model in the face of disruptive technology it had ironically invented – digital photography. Steve Sasson, the Kodak engineer who invented the first digital camera in 1975, characterised the initial corporate response to his invention this way: "But it was filmless photography, so management's reaction was, 'that's cute – but don't tell anyone about it.'"

For many people, change isn't easy.

Over the past few years, I've been invited to speak to people in organisations all around the world, to empower staff with the tools and strategies to lead and deal positively with change:

- The semiconductor organisation needing to change its culture so employees are more innovative and proactive about managing quality.

- The oil and gas logistics company that has seen profits wiped out over the past two years and needs to diversify its operations to stay relevant.

- Councils across Australia who are going through amalgamation or into a "shared services" model, or simply have to become significantly more customer-centric.

- The legal firm that has gone through a period of significant growth and needs their senior staff to focus more on developing their team and growing the business, beyond meeting their personal billable utilisation targets.

In all these situations, the managers are invariably stressed out about how to keep staff engaged, deal with poor staff morale, or handle attrition (which is having a grave impact on productivity), and how to motivate staff so the organisation can avoid implementing even more dramatic cost-saving measures.

We're generally pretty ok with changes that we initiate, even those that are significantly disruptive. For me personally, this would have included decisions such as moving to Australia for my higher school and tertiary education, accepting my first job offer to work for the late Professor Cyril Brookes, marrying Sue, deciding to settle down in Australia, starting a family, moving to the Silicon Valley, moving back to Australia, starting out at IBM, moving to a better neighbourhood, taking up a promotion or expanded role, and changing careers altogether to pursue my present vocation. The changes most of us struggle with tend to be those we were not expecting and that we feel have been forced upon us against our will. For me, the two that stand out are the organisational restructure I went through at IBM and the day I learned that my brother Gary was diagnosed with a mental illness. Just like the other changes, both these changes and how I responded to them would dramatically alter the course of my life.

Reflection

Just for a moment, pause and reflect on the following. Think of changes that have occurred in your life that you were able to manage pretty well. What did these changes have in common?

Now think of several changes that occurred that were sources of tremendous stress for you. What did these changes have in common?

What is it that makes such change so challenging for most?

When I asked this question of my workshop participants over the course of the past decade, the answer was invariably the same *"fear of the unknown"* and our perception that the change represents a threat in some way to our sense of security, status, community, or general well-being.

The hardest part about change really isn't so much about the change in role or routine or having to learn to do new things differently, but about dealing with the **emotions** that arise during times of change.

For instance, my team's restructure in 2001 required my staff and I to take on new roles that involved developing new competencies and doing things differently. We were moving from a product/geographic centric organisation to one that was solution focussed. Instead of being structured by region (North, South, Central) and within each region, by product teams (Lotus, Tivoli, WebSphere, DB2), we were moving towards a leaner, more solution-centric organisation (knowledge management solutions, collaboration solutions, portal solutions, etc.) better aligned to meet the needs of our customers.

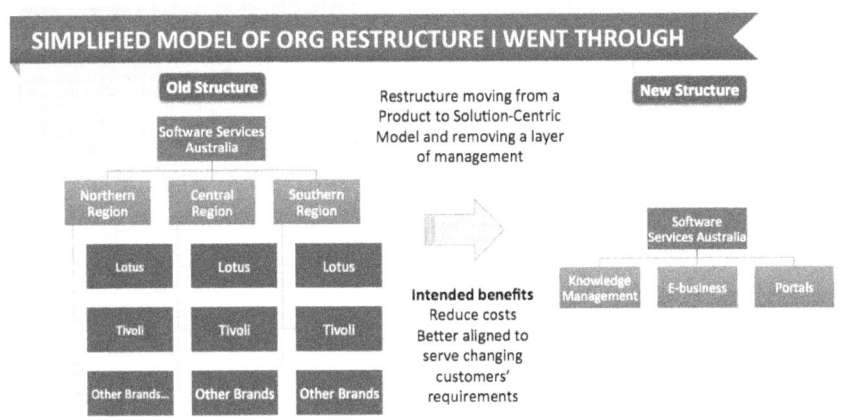

Figure 1 - Simplified model of the restructure I went through

Whereas in the past, selling predominantly involved presenting features, functions and benefits of our latest product releases to our customers (typically the Chief Information Officer), our sales force now needed to reinvent themselves to firstly learn about the new solutions we could offer, establish relationships with new buyers (the "business" as opposed to the IT side of the customer), be able to master interviewing skills to understand the problems the business were facing, and then be able to explain how our solutions could help the customer with their issues.

Our consultants (instead of being experts in a specific technology) had to transform themselves so they could understand our new solutions and learn how to put them together for our customers using a variety of our different products. In both scenarios, getting the new skills was challenging, but not half as challenging as overcoming the fear, anxiety, stress and uncertainty of the unknown.

Remember that the results we wish to get in our lives (in the example above, being regarded as a solutions oriented organisation, a market leader in e-business solutions, being more cost effective and enhancing shareholder returns in the process) are determined largely by our actions. Just as importantly, realise that the actions we take are impacted by how we *feel* - the emotional state we're in.

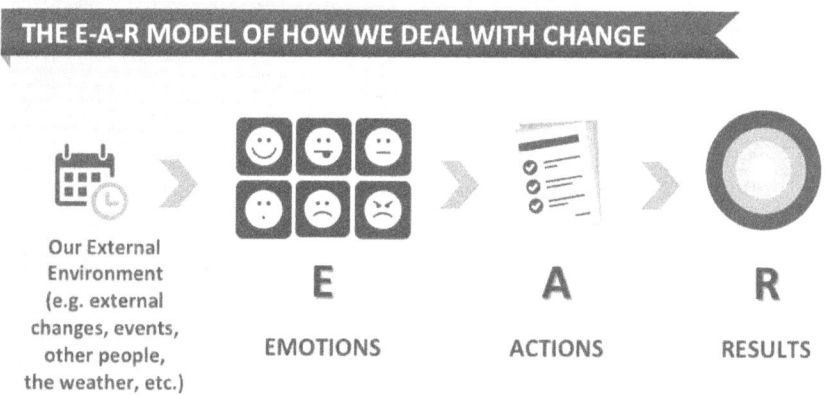

Figure 2 – The E-A-R model of how we deal with change

If we're enthusiastic, passionate, and motivated by the change, and put these emotions into what we do, chances are high that we'll be able to master the new skills demanded by the new state, put them into practise and deliver the results. However, even if we had the skills and know-how required to make the transition to a new role, if we weren't able to turn fear, stress and anxiety into enthusiasm, optimism, and motivation, we wouldn't be able to fulfil the potential that already lies within us. Fear and uncertainty can debilitate us and increase our stress levels to the point of paralysis. This can result in decisions that are ineffective at best and destructive at worst.

Mastering change starts first with understanding, managing and mastering our emotions during times of change. This is why learning to read, control, manage and influence our emotional state is pivotal to our ability to deal with change.

Your EQ is the Foundation of your Resilience

"To the degree that our emotions get in the way of, or enhance our ability to think and plan, to pursue training for a distant goal, to solve problems and the like, they define the limits of our capacity to use our innate mental abilities, and so determine how we do in life. And to the degree to which we are motivated by feelings of enthusiasm and pleasure in what we do — or even by an optimal degree of anxiety — they propel us to accomplishment. It is in this sense that emotional intelligence is a master aptitude, a capacity that profoundly affects all other abilities, either facilitating or interfering with them."

— Daniel Goleman

What is it that affects our emotions? How can we create emotional states that serve us during times of change – emotional states such as optimism, joy, passion, enthusiasm and faith rather than be debilitated by fear, anxiety, guilt, hurt and frustration?

[2]The ability to read, control, manage, and influence our emotional state and that of others is what Professors Peter Salovey (Yale University) and John D. Mayer (University of New Hampshire) refer to as our

emotional intelligence (EI), which is measured by our emotional quotient (EQ).

Traditionally, when most people think about intelligence, we think about a narrow realm of intelligence called our cognitive intelligence (measured by our IQ) - our ability to read, write, comprehend, do math and solve problems. Literacy, numeracy and ICT still form the foundation of many nations' education systems, and "smart" folks are defined as those with high Mensa scores and by the level of their academic qualifications. While most advanced economies in the world today have high literacy and numeracy levels, it's easy to forget that as recently as 40-50 years ago, as much as 50% of the population of developing countries of the day such as Singapore, Malaysia, and the UAE, had had little formal education. The key to getting out of the poverty cycle and experiencing economic growth was to educate the masses and get them into employment.

Much of the education emphasis today (particularly in nations that as recently as 50 years ago were still developing economies), remains focussed on getting people employed, as opposed to giving them the wisdom to deal with life. There remains a significant emphasis on developing one's cognitive intelligence since this is a foundation for specialist technical skills — how to be a doctor, plumber, mechanic, accountant, engineer, etc. Success measured by academic grades often drives the focus of teaching, which means there isn't enough time to equip people with life skills like resilience and how to thrive in times of change, particularly when a person's technical skills may be obsolete the moment they step out of tertiary schooling. The pressure for academic excellence, rather than life skills like learning to lead, deal with stress, and relate to others, often meant that someone with a great capacity to retain and regurgitate copious amounts of information straight from the textbooks, could make it to the top. When you couple a system where schools are given a grading (e.g. "selective" versus "non-selective") and classes are streamed with a "winner takes all", zero-sum mindset, very often, what you get is a situation where the brightest are "lone wolf" high achievers who lack the skills to relate to others and communicate effectively. This system breeds perfectionists who are often afraid to fail, and when they do face setbacks, the pressure that comes from societal expectations can be overwhelming. This was the environment I was brought up in.

My life-changing experience in 2001 taught me that you can have great cognitive intelligence, the most wonderful academic qualifications behind you, and a strong CV, but it counts for nothing if you're unable to turn frustration, anxiety, lethargy and fear into passion, motivation, faith, and optimism.

Emotional Self-Awareness

Salovey and Mayer's research[3] showed that people with a high level of emotional intelligence were more effective, made better leaders, were better adjusted, were more resilient and happier than those without. [4]In 1996, Harvard Professor Daniel Goleman built on the work of Salovey and Mayer, and brought emotional intelligence to the mainstream when he published the findings of his research in the book "Emotional Intelligence: Why it can matter more than IQ". This publication shot to the top of the bestseller list and stayed there for months.

Goleman's research showed that people who were the finest leaders were not just adaptable, but they were often change catalysts (think Steve Jobs, Elon Musk, Margaret Thatcher, Oprah Winfrey, Mahatma Gandhi, Nelson Mandela, Richard Branson). This ability was built on a foundation of optimism, emotional self-control, achievement orientation, plus a tendency to take initiative, have empathy, be service oriented, and be socially aware. These traits in turn were developed on a foundation of self-awareness. He called these traits emotional competencies, and through the use of personal and 360 assessment tools, we can actually measure our emotional intelligence today.

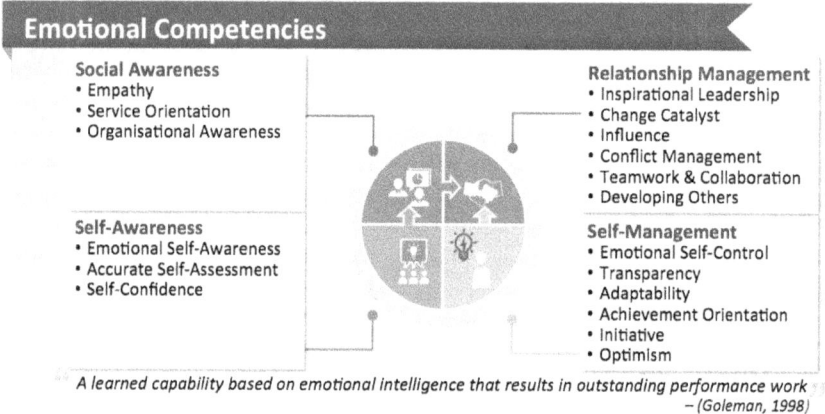

Figure 3 - Emotional Competencies and Resilience

In order to influence my team to achieve our ideal incomes from the change during the tumultuous period from 2001, I needed to first be aware that fear, uncertainty, doubt, and frustration were affecting my confidence, energy levels, and actions. I was low on energy, often put up a brave front, dragged my heels to work, sought the solace of my cubicle and chose to "lay low", licking my wounds. My attitude was,

"I thought I was paid to lead. Given I was not even consulted about this, my opinion obviously doesn't matter. That being the case, I'll just focus on doing my job." My actions and performance during that period would have reflected that of an individual contributor rather than a senior manager.

It would also have been helpful for me to know that my response was having a negative impact on the emotional states of others around me. Studies on communication by Professor Albert Mehrabian[5] have shown that the choice of words we use to express ourselves is just 7% of the message pertaining to feelings and attitudes, with the remaining 93% being reflected by how we say what we say (tone and body language), and a full 55% coming from non-verbal cues. My team would have no doubt been impacted by the negative body language and energy I was putting out. When they needed me to provide them with a sense of direction and certainty, I went AWOL. This would have hurt them deeply, and it certainly had a significant impact on my level of self-confidence and self-esteem.

I needed to first be aware of this, then be able to control and alter my emotional states to be more dynamic, positive, optimistic, and determined about the change. That was during a period I now call my "B-EQ" ("before EQ") days.

Exercising Emotional Self-Awareness

"The quality of your life is the quality of the emotions you consistently experience"

— Tony Robbins

So what is emotional self-awareness? Simply, it is the ability to understand and recognise how you're feeling, and to be aware of how those feelings are impacting your thinking and actions[6]. My life changed the moment I realised this and learned the levers I could use to change my emotional state from any undesired state to one of my preference at will. This is a foundational mind-set of the resilient - the belief that while **you may not have the power to decide what happens around you,** *you and you alone* **have the power to choose how to think and feel about it and thus the actions and results you get.**

So right at this moment, take note of how you're feeling. On a scale of 1-10, what's your level of energy? Energy is a form of emotion. If you'd like to predict in advance how well you're going to do in any situation or time of change, the key piece of data you need right now is how you're **feeling**. If you're committed to a level 10 outcome, you'd want your energy to be at level 10. Anything lower than this and you're settling for a sub-par performance and outcome.

Knowing and reading how you're feeling right now means that you're exercising your emotional self-awareness. Being aware of your emotional state and your ability to then change that state to one that helps you with your ideal outcomes, is a key habit that distinguishes resilient people from those who are less so.

From this moment on, be more attentive to how you're feeling at any one time. Take time out to reflect and take stock of how you feel. Know that some emotional states are helpful to actions you need to take to demonstrate resilience and optimism and some are not. Learning to pause, reflect, put a label on how you're feeling (without reacting to the emotion) and if required, change your emotional state to one that is more reflective of resilient, optimistic behaviour will help you strengthen emotional self-awareness over time.

Activity - Empowering and disempowering emotions

Let's take an inventory of the emotions you experienced over the course of the past week. Write down a list of all these emotions either using a note pad or in the accompanying workbook. There are literally thousands of words that describe emotions in the dictionary. A sample of some common words is presented below. For now, don't judge them. Just write them down as quickly as possible.

Sample Emotions

Tertiary Emotions	Secondary Emotion	Primary Emotion
Adoration, affection, love, fondness, liking, attraction, caring, tenderness, compassion, sentimentality	Affection	Love
Arousal, desire, lust, passion, infatuation	Lust	
Joviality, joy, delight, enjoyment, gladness, happiness, jubilation, elation, satisfaction, ecstasy, euphoria	Cheerfulness	Joy
Enthusiasm, zeal, zest, excitement, thrill, exhilaration	Zest	
Contentment, pleasure	Contentment	
Pride, triumph	Pride	
Eagerness, hope, optimism	Optimism	
Enthrallment, rapture	Enthrallment	
Relief	Relief	

Tertiary Emotions	Secondary Emotion	Primary Emotion
Amazement, surprise, astonishment, aggravation, irritation, agitation	Surprise	Surprise
Annoyance, grouchiness, grumpiness	Irritation	
Exasperation, frustration	Exasperation	Anger
Anger, rage, outrage, fury, wrath, hostility, ferocity, bitterness, hate, loathing, scorn, spite, vengefulness, dislike, resentment	Rage	
Disgust, revulsion, contempt	Disgust	
Envy, jealousy	Envy	
Torment	Torment	
Agony, suffering, hurt, anguish	Suffering	
Depression, despair, hopelessness, gloom, glumness, sadness, unhappiness, grief, sorrow, woe, misery, melancholy	Sadness	Sadness
Dismay, disappointment, displeasure	Disappointment	
Guilt, shame, regret, remorse	Shame	

Tertiary Emotions	Secondary Emotion	Primary Emotion
Alienation, isolation, neglect, loneliness, rejection, homesickness, defeat, dejection, insecurity, embarrassment, humiliation, insult	Neglect	Sadness
Pity, sympathy	Sympathy	
Alarm, shock, fear, fright, horror, terror, panic, hysteria, mortification	Horror	Fear
Anxiety, nervousness, tenseness, uneasiness, apprehension, worry, distress, dread	Nervousness	

Source: Parrott, W. (2001), Emotions in Social Psychology, Psychology Press, Philadelphia

Table 1 - Range of Emotions

Know that each of the emotions we experience serves a purpose. There are no "good" or "bad" emotions. Fear is not a helpful emotional state to be in if it prevents you from speaking up, asserting yourself, or dealing constructively with conflict. But it certainly serves us when it prevents us from jumping off a cliff. In the context of resilience and dealing positively with change, there are only what I call *empowering* or *disempowering* emotions.

To "empower" is to give you the feeling that you're powerful from within. To be in an empowered state is to experience one or more emotions that best support the actions you need to take to achieve the ideal outcomes you seek from any situation. I also call these emotions "energy giving" emotions. Such emotions are usually derivatives of the primary emotion called "love" — enthusiasm, passion, optimism, faith, hope, gratitude, confidence, etc. To feel disempowered means you feel in some way helpless, or are experiencing an emotional state that prevents you from achieving the ideal desired outcome in any situation. I call these emotions "energy taking" emotions. Being in such states drains you of the energy you need to get the best outcomes from the situation. Such emotions are usually derivative of the primary emotion called "fear" — anxiety, frustration, anger, hurt, guilt, depression, sadness, etc.

Which category of emotions would serve you best during times of change? Empowering, energy-giving, love emotions or disempowering, energy-taking, fear emotions?

During the time of my organisational restructure at IBM, filling my life with enthusiasm, strength and faith would have certainly empowered me much more than frustration, anger and hurt.

So another important element of emotional self-awareness is our ability to distinguish between those that empower us, and those that disempower us when it comes to achieving the ideal outcomes we seek in that particular situation.

Activity

For each of the emotions you have listed in the previous exercise, put a circle around those you deem to be empowering.

Look at the list of emotions you've put together. Do you have more empowering or disempowering emotions on that list? During times of change, which emotions help you get ideal outcomes, and which don't?

Cultivating Power Emotional Tools

When I did this exercise, I realised that when I was struggling to adapt, I was experiencing more disempowering emotions than I did empowering ones. To be resilient and thrive through the change meant first learning how to summon up any empowering emotional state I wanted at will. I made a critical decision then that would have a tremendous flow on effect on my life, my level of resilience and that of others around my circle of influence. I decided that I would work hard to consciously create and experience four emotional states that I call my Power Emotional Tools (PETs) of resilience. These PETs were **Courage**, **Faith**, **Love** and **Fun**.

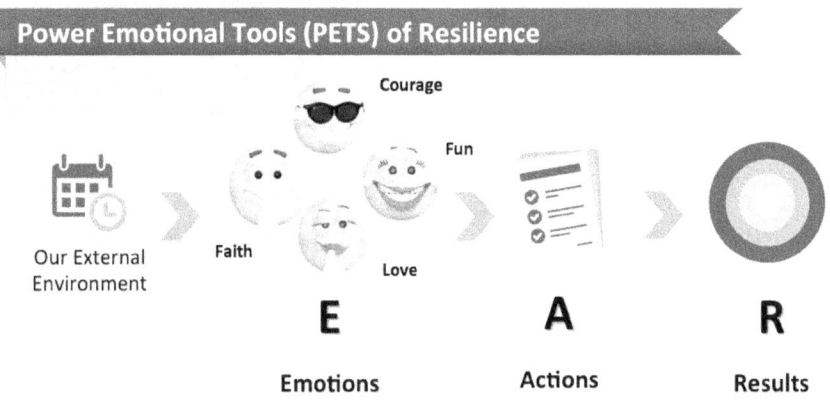

Figure 4 - The Power Emotional Tools (PETs) I Chose

Courage

"Courage is not the absence of fear but rather the judgement that something else is more important than fear. The brave may not live forever, but the cautious do not live at all."

- Ambrose Redmoon

I chose courage because I realised that the experience I went through was due not so much to what happened but to the state of fear and uncertainty I would invariably slip into during moments of uncertainty. One of the traits I've observed about people who are truly adaptable is that <u>they are comfortable being vulnerable</u>. Imagine that instead of getting into paralysis mode (by analysis), I had responded with gratitude, faith, and courage and said this:

"Keith, thanks for having the courtesy to call me directly rather than me getting this message second-hand through others. I know how busy you are and I'm grateful for your call. What you're saying to me is incredibly important. Could you give me a few minutes to pull the car over and give you my undivided attention?

Keith, from your position, you're probably seeing threats, issues and challenges with the way our organisation is presently being structured. Could you fill me in please with what those threats and challenges are? What would be the ultimate consequences to our business and our team if the structure remained unchanged two, three and five years from now?

What if we were successful in making this transition? How would that benefit our team, our business and our customers?

Also, the 30% of my team that are being redeployed will need help. What resources can you offer me to ensure they get all the support they need during this challenging period? The rest of my team will also be impacted by this. What resources can you offer me to help them stay focussed and determined about achieving our ideal outcomes this year?

We'll be going through a challenging period. Know that you can count on me to keep the ship steady during these turbulent times. I'd love to contribute to defining the ideal new structure to ensure it meets with your ideal outcomes. Let me know what I can do."

Imagine if I'd had the self-confidence and communication skills to do that. What do you think the next two years of my life would have been like?

What prevented me from doing that? Fear. Fear of being vulnerable, of appearing naïve, of asking the wrong questions. Heed the words of Brene Brown, who says, "Embracing our vulnerabilities is risky but not nearly as dangerous as giving up on love and belonging and joy — the experiences that make us the most vulnerable. Only when we are brave enough to explore the darkness will we discover the infinite power of our light.[7]"

Faith

"Faith consists in believing when it is beyond the power of reason to believe." — Voltaire

I chose faith because it underpins one of the most common traits of winners – achievement-orientation. Winners are constantly setting goals they're excited about and then pursuing them with all their might in spite of the uncertainty. Think about the Olympians. For four long years, they sacrifice, overcome great adversity and exercise great discipline in the quest of an ideal they've deemed worthy, with no guarantee of success. All it takes is one major injury or setback outside their control and it could be the end of their dream. Yet, they stay the course, undeterred, inspiring all of us in the process.

On a recent flight home, I chose to watch the autobiographical documentary about the journey of Usain Bolt, considered one of the greatest track-and-field athletes of all time. He won three gold medals in the prized events of the 100-metre, 200-metre and 4 x 100-metre relay at three consecutive Olympics. This feat is certainly going to take some beating. It's an extraordinary account of an exceptional individual who in spite of injuries, countless setbacks and the tremendous sacrifices and pain endured (one small example — imagine having to sit in an ice-bath after every single training session over all those years), set bigger and more challenging goals regularly and in the process, defied both age and the doubters to remind us of the power of faith and how incredibly resilient all of us can be.

All the great leaders have this trait.

I will forever be grateful to my forefather who left the safety of his village in China in a rickety boat more than a century ago, and headed towards what he must have heard was the land of promise and opportunity (Malaysia) with faith as his shield and life-jacket.

I can only imagine his fear and trepidation – after all, I'm sure he'd have heard all about the dangers of unpredictable tides, currents, and pirates who preyed on such travellers. And yet, this man's decision would have been made not in the absence of fear, but out of his commitment to create a brighter future for his family. Today, my family and I get to enjoy a most blessed life in Australia, the land of opportunity. I remind my children constantly to never take for granted the great life we have and to honour the sacrifices and faith of our forefathers by being role models of this faith. To constantly pursue their dreams and to use their talents to make the biggest difference they can to the lives of others, and in the course of that, explore and fulfil their highest potential.

If you'd asked me back in 2001 where I saw myself in five years, I'd have said, "It depends on the restructure." I had the victim-mentality of a whiner and was a model of learned helplessness. "I have no power to control my destiny — the environment is in charge — so why set myself up for failure by setting goals I cannot achieve?"

This level of thinking only made me feel disempowered and trapped. I thought a good job, position, and money would make me secure and give me freedom. But the more I made, the more my "nice-to-haves" had become "wants" and then "needs" and the more attached I was to the trappings of my lifestyle. I couldn't envisage risking losing anything I had worked so hard to create and the embarrassment and sense of failure I might get as a result. My attachment to such trappings had become my handcuffs to a job I was no longer passionate about. To experience true freedom, I knew the answer lay not in my circumstances but in tapping into the power of faith.

My definition of faith (some call it optimism) is, "the feeling that comes from having a deep trust that everything that happens, happens for a good reason and that is intended to help me in some way. Sometimes these reasons only become obvious in the future. And if I do everything I can with what I've got and with the greater good in mind, things will work out fine."

All of us exercise faith in some manner each and every day. For those of us who drive, every time we get out on the road, we exercise faith — that no incoming vehicle will come onto our side of the road and take us out. Without faith, how much freedom would we have? When we send our kids to school, we're exercising faith that they'll be safe and secure in the presence of strangers. And yet, I've learned that I was being *selective* in demonstrating faith. In my time of great uncertainty, I was not willing to tap into faith, rather relying on rational or logical thought for my decisions: "Can I afford to? Do I have the skills to? Is this the right time?" I chose faith because often, the best decisions are made by listening to our inner voice, and tapping into the realm of our intuition, rather than relying on logic. I chose faith because I valued this thing called freedom.

Fun

"While you're going through this process of trying to find the satisfaction in your work, pretend you feel satisfied. Tell yourself you had a good day. Walk through the corridors with a smile rather than a scowl. Your positive energy will radiate. If you act like you're having fun, you'll find you are having fun."

— Jean Chatzky

I chose fun because at that time of my life, I realised I was taking things way too seriously. Perhaps that came from a time in my youth when I decided that if I did not present myself as a serious young man, I couldn't expect others to treat me seriously. I still remember as a school prefect in my middle school years, I consciously chose to wear a frown as I walked around the school, modelling those whose role was to instil discipline in others. This had become a habit I brought into my professional life.

Looking back, this would be the start of the mask I'd wear to hide the impish playfulness that I had inside of me – the "inner child" that lies in each and every one of us. I've always admired those who could laugh at themselves and the stuff life throws at them, not taking themselves and things too seriously during times of adversity. This is, in fact, one of the most empowering resources you can tap into to be resilient.

I decided then that life was too short not to have fun every day and in every way.

Love

I chose love, quite frankly, out of fear. Fear that in making the cultivation of the other three PETs a priority, I might somehow lose sight of being a loving person. So love became my fourth PET. Love is this amazing emotion that encompasses all forms of positive energy — hope, faith, gratitude. I learned that in times of great uncertainty, if I could draw on a faith that everything that happens has love as its source and then decide to let my love for others and myself drive my decision, those decisions would always be the right ones to make.

Making a conscious choice to *be* one of those PETs as often as I could was the start of my journey to recovery and also the start of living a life of fulfilment.

Today, I can say that my life is considerably more filled with courage, faith, love and fun. I have found that with these PETs, changes and challenges have simply become opportunities for adventure, learning, loving and giving even more. And that has made my life considerably more fulfilling.

Action Steps and Reflection

1. It's now your turn to pick your PETs. Which four emotional states will you DECIDE today, to experience more often and with greater intensity, that will help you not only to be more resilient but to thrive through change?

2. Imagine experiencing those states with greater regularity and depth, how would that benefit you?

3. What else becomes possible?

4. Who else would benefit from you being in those states more often? In what way?

5. Take this 10-day challenge – consciously choose to put a smile on the face of at least three people you meet every day.

6. What could you do to introduce more fun and spontaneity into everything you do? What could you spontaneously decide to do

today that's fun for you and will make a positive difference to someone else?

7. Reflect on the following: If fear wasn't present, what are three things you'd like to achieve this year that would make it a great year for you and others around you?

CHAPTER 4

Be the Change

You have the power to choose your response to change

It's not the change, but the meaning you give to the change that affects your feelings, actions and outcomes

Press the PAUSE button whenever you feel disempowered

Be aware of the meaning you are giving to the change

Choose a meaning that creates the empowering emotional states you want

Choose to respond and not react to change

Whenever you're feeling disempowered, learn to master the magic phrase "tell me more"

Exercise your self-awareness, imagination, conscience and independent will

"People are always blaming their circumstances for what they are. I don't believe in circumstances. The people who get on in this world are the people who get up and look for the circumstances they want, and if they can't find them, make them." — George Bernard Shaw

"Be. Do. Live." — Rajeev Dewan

Going Beyond Blame

Imagine if your life was filled with the PETs you've chosen. Imagine being able to create such emotional states at will. How would life be for you? How resilient would you be? In this and the next couple of chapters, you'll learn how to create any emotional state you want whenever you want.

In order to learn these strategies, it's important for us to understand what it is that affects our emotional states.

Many who are asked this question point to external factors – their environment, circumstances, or the people around them. If you had asked me back in my darkest period what was causing me to lack energy and drive, I would have put the blame solely on the situation I was in. *"The restructure took the wind off my sails. It's my management and the stifling culture of control."*

How often have we heard responses like this?

- You should meet my husband/wife/mother-in-law/children. Then you'll know why I'm so miserable.

- It's the darned government. All politics. Taxing us more and giving us less.

- It's the weather.

Whiners see themselves as victims of their circumstances. Winners believe that they have the power within themselves to become masters of their destiny.

Whiners lay blame for their misery on everything around them - things that are not within their control. **Winners understand that the environment and other people can affect the way they feel, but it doesn't *determine* the way they feel.** They cannot control their environment but they have total control over how they choose to respond to it.

Through the four key gifts that humankind (as a primate species) is uniquely endowed with - self-awareness, imagination, conscience, and independent will — we can choose our emotional response to every situation. More on these gifts later.

But first, a quick lesson on how the brain works. Why is it that for many, an instinctive first emotional response to uncertainty is fear?

Have you ever considered what the most basic function of the brain is? Yes, you have the right answer – **survival**. The brain in its present model is about 40,000 to 60,000 years old — when we first became what the scientists call homo sapiens. While I spent many years learning how to master the workings of the humble computer, I wish I'd learned much earlier how to master the most powerful computer ever – our human brain.

The original operating system of the brain is pretty basic. In simple terms, it's a one-line command – *"eat lunch, don't be lunch"*. So back when we were cave dwellers, when we felt the tremors on the ground and heard the frightened sounds of creatures fleeing for their lives and sensed that a predator could be approaching, our senses (the input device) would send signals to our brain (our computer) that say "danger approaching".

Figure 5 - The flight or fight response

This signal would be transmitted to the part of the brain (CPU or central processing unit) that processes danger signals called the amygdala. Like the chip in the computer that deals with the fan overheating, the amygdala is akin to the crisis command centre. Its function is to set off alarm signals that activate the nervous system into full battle ("freeze, flight or fight") readiness. It does this by inducing a hormone called cortisol. [9]Cortisol is also known as the stress hormone. It's a highly concentrated dose of glucose — when cortisol is present, your senses and system are in high alert. Your heart races, blood pressure rises, muscles become tense. Fear is at an all-time high.

Have you ever seen that program on National Geographic — a flock of gazelle grazing peacefully in the savannahs of Africa? It's a picturesque, peaceful, beautiful day. Suddenly, one of the gazelle detects rustling through the bushes. A predator is near. Its instinctive response is to raise its head, its ears fully cocked, its nostrils flared, its muscles taut. This is called the "freeze" response. At this moment, this gazelle can kick harder, run faster, and leap higher than it ever has before. This is nature's function for cortisol — a powerful, survival mechanism, and a really important and handy hormone to have in our system.

Here's the downside of having too much cortisol. When cortisol is the predominant hormone in our system, and fear the primary emotion, all our other metabolic systems with the function to serve *growth* — to regenerate and produce healthy new muscle tissue, our libido, etc. - are shut down. The brain's logic works like this - who needs longer toe and fingernails, facial hair, or regenerated muscle tissue when our life is at stake? In other words, when cortisol floods our system, we're in survival mode. However, being in survival mode simply means we're degenerating physically. If we are not growing, we're dying. Simple as that.

> *"If you're standing still, you're moving backwards."*
>
> *— Wayne Bennett, famous Australian rugby league coach*

Fast forward to today. Our brain structure and systems are pretty much unchanged. Many of the things that increase our cortisol levels and thus our fear and stress levels are subconscious reactions to situations that are hardly life-threatening — a terse email from a colleague, running late for a meeting or taking the kids to school, children not completing their homework, someone not allowing you into their lane despite your signals, your mum complaining about you not visiting her often enough, even workplace changes!

Unlike many decades and centuries ago, today, we live in an unprecedented period of empowerment, freedom, security and peace.

Yet our brain's operating system remains largely unchanged and **conditioned** by previous generations when survival was the name of the game. Just one generation ago, my dad lost two siblings before the age of five. This was a time when medicine was not quite as advanced as it is today. Both died of influenza. I lived a very sheltered life growing up. "Don't go out to play when it's raining — you might catch the flu. Don't leave the table until you've eaten every last morsel – you don't know when the next meal might be here." And for many of us in this present generation, where we're enjoying relative security, empowerment, wealth, access to knowledge and advances in medication, we still habitually get unduly stressed when for instance, our kids don't get the grades we feel they're capable of, or have missed a meal.

When I received that phone call that fateful morning, really, what's the worst that could have happened? I could have lost my job. It might take me several months to find another. Perhaps I might need to get on the dole and rely on a government payout for a while. But that's hardly life-threatening. And yet, my days were filled with fear, anxiety and stress.

Failure to be aware of and manage an amygdala that's on overdrive means our bodies are often at high stress levels — and degenerating. This is literally killing us every day. Today's major, non-accident related killers in the US are heart disease, cancer, chronic lower respiratory diseases, stroke, Alzheimer's disease and diabetes. These conditions are all lifestyle diseases with strong links to high stress levels being a major contributor.

So, the first thing to note is that if your common emotional response to change or uncertainty is fear, or any of its other manifestations in what's been documented as the "Kubler-Ross Emotional Cycle of Change" — denial, anger, shock, guilt, depression — know that this is common and natural, and there is nothing wrong with you. You're most definitely not alone in the human conditioning of reactively experiencing fear in times of change.

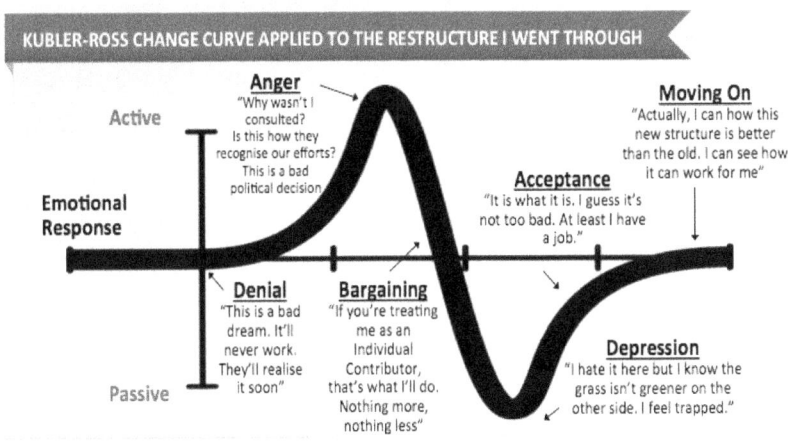

Figure 6 - The cycle of emotions we go through during times of change

Our brain today has developed what's called a "negativity bias" — a tendency to focus more heavily and exaggerate the possible threats and dangers posed by a situation, than it needs to. Being aware of this negativity bias and reconditioning our brain so that it stays much calmer and rational in times of stress is the key to being more adaptable and resilient.

Realise that when we are fearful, we get into what I call a state of high emotion. When we're in a state of high emotion, we often make decisions and react in ways we often later regret. Have you ever said or done something instinctively when you felt threatened, angry or hurt and later regretted it? All of us have been there, done that. Remember this phrase — *"when emotion is high, intelligence is low"*. We become victims of a syndrome called the "amygdala hijack", where rational thought gets thrown out the window.

Amygdala hijack is a term coined by Daniel Goleman in his 1996 book *Emotional Intelligence: Why It Can Matter More Than IQ*. Drawing on the work of Joseph E. LeDoux, Goleman uses the term to describe emotional responses from people which are immediate and overwhelming, and out of measure with the actual stimulus because it has triggered a much more significant emotional threat.

Pressing the PAUSE button

So, in times of uncertainty, the first key step is to remember **not** to react. The moment you're aware that you're feeling a form of fear and the situation is **not** life threatening, push the PAUSE button and take time out to reflect.

Let me share with you a personal anecdote of how I applied this in a way that would forever change the way I reacted to situations.

I have three wonderful children who mean the world to me. Two sons and a daughter. Our sons went to a school that prided itself in instilling in its students a strong sense of core values and discipline. Kids went to school in a jacket and tie, no metal adornments were allowed (earrings, etc.), no tattoos, and there were strict rules around hair length and colour. If you were late to school more than three times in a semester, you'd be held back on Friday afternoon for detention.

Aaron is my second son. He's 21 today, completing a degree in media and marketing at Macquarie University and works as an Apple Genius four days a week. Aaron didn't particularly enjoy his early years at this school, and he'd often come home complaining about how the school was really rigid and outdated in its rules.

Aaron has always been a kind-hearted kid and used to really love dance – hip hop was his thing. He couldn't stand math — 10 minutes of math homework would drive him nuts — but with hip hop dance, he could do this for hours. Loved it. But I must admit his teenage years were often a challenge to his "old school" parents. I remember him coming home one day — he was 13 then — and saying, "Dad, I'd like to dye my hair." Or "I'd like to have an earring." Stuff that we knew would violate the school rules and get him into trouble.

During his early secondary school years, Aaron's academic results were a source of great anxiety and concern for his parents who grew up in an era and country (Malaysia) where getting good grades and a university degree meant everything — certainly a ticket to a white collar job that would give you greater security. In Malaysia, the gulf in financial remuneration between white and blue-collar jobs is huge. No degree and you're doomed to a life of hardship, conjuring up images of back-breaking labour under the hot sun and taking home a pittance after a hard day's work. Blue-collar jobs were perceived to be for those who didn't have the smarts. It would certainly be a source of great embarrassment for families with white-collar parents to have children ending up with blue-collar jobs.

So knowing how his results were, and how much he hated school, we also associated him getting into disciplinary trouble at school with making such matters even worse. And so, his requests would typically be greeted with a reactive and stern "No!" I still remember those occasions when he'd come home from school in a bad mood complaining how he had been held back for Friday afternoon detention for getting in two minutes after the school bell. His laments of, "I hate my school" would often make us feel helpless and stressed. We were sending him to what we felt was the best school we could afford and yet, he was having what we felt was the most miserable experience and not getting the results we felt he was capable of.

One day several years ago, six weeks into his Higher School Certificate ("A"-levels) year — in Australia, this is the final year of high school - he came to me and said, "Dad, what would you say if I said I was thinking of shaving my head?"

Immediately, I felt my stress and gastric juice levels rise, my amygdala going on over-drive. My mind went through this self-talk:

"Son, when are you going to grow up? Just a few months ago, you came home complaining about the Friday afternoon detention and how your teachers are so inflexible. Can't you see that *you* are the source of the problem? You know this is against the school rules."

Remember, it's not what happens that affects the way we feel, but the meaning (our "Thoughts") we give to what happens. And our emotions drive our behaviour and thus our results.

This situation would have, in what I call the B-EQ (before I learned about EQ) period of my life, resulted in me losing my cool and saying, "I don't care what you do when you're 21 and when you may no longer be living under my roof. Right now, just do what I say and focus on your studies OK? That's NOT ON!" And guess what the result would have been? Yes, he might have gone ahead and shaved his head anyway. And guess how much tension that would have created in the household the next few months? What would the level of trust be between us? How willing might he be to come to me for my opinion in future? I think you know what the answer is.

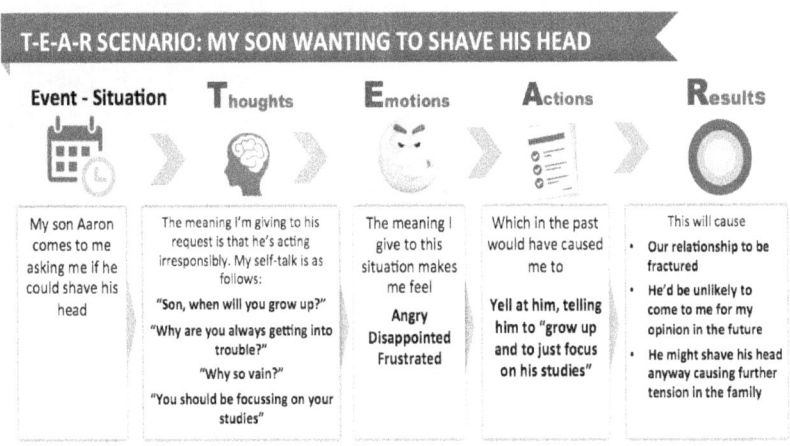

Figure 7 - Understanding TEAR and how it affects our outcomes

Ever since I've practised the "begin with the ideal end in mind" habit in my life I've known that when I get to age 60, I know exactly what I'd ideally like for my children to say if they were invited to give a speech about their dad on his birthday. It would be something along these lines.

"I'm living the life of my dreams using my talents to the max to make the biggest difference to the lives of others around me. I couldn't be happier. My dad gave me permission to do so, mostly by the example he led. My dad was always busy, but never too busy for me when it mattered. He always believed in me. He made me feel better about myself when I was around him. He's one of the happiest people I know."

I've decided that achieving this would mean I did something right as a parent, which for me is the most important role in my life and also my greatest privilege. It would also be a barometer of the quality of my relationship with my kids, who I treasure dearly. But to achieve this would be the result of an accumulation of every single interaction I have with them — be it a WhatsApp chat, phone call or face-to-face session.

So I decided some years ago that in every interaction I would have with my children, unless their non-compliance would endanger their lives or others around them, **my top two priority outcomes would be to strengthen our mutual relationship and trust, and make them feel even better about themselves**. Getting them to take my advice would be a third outcome, knowing that was something I could influence but could not control. I could lead a horse to water but I couldn't make it drink. I knew that if I did what was right 99% of the time, the time when I really needed them to heed my advice, I could simply say, "Son, I really need you to trust me on this. Just do as I suggest" and they'd respect that because they'd know I had their best interests at heart.

Now, the "inner chat" I was having that was riling me up was happening in a matter of microseconds in my brain. Applying my self-awareness (feeling disempowering emotions welling up) and imagination (knowing my reactive response would create a result *I didn't want*, and imagining what I really wanted instead), I immediately put a smile on my face, straightened my posture, took a deep, calming breath, leaned forward, reached out my right hand with a welcoming gesture and calmly said, "tell me more". Three magical words. This simple technique (for dealing with tension and conflict) has transformed how I respond to situations, conflict and people around me. Master this technique and I believe it will also do wonders for your relationships!

Figure 8 - "Tell me more"

Aaron said, "Dad, for the last six weeks, one of my good friends, Johnny hasn't been coming to school. We've been trying to reach him – his Facebook page, phone calls, text messages – but not getting any replies. Whenever we asked our teachers about Johnny, they seemed cagey and strangely evasive. This morning, we finally learned why.

Johnny came to school. He's lost all his hair, dad. Turns out, he was recently diagnosed with Hodgkin's Lymphoma. He's been through several bouts of chemotherapy that has caused him to lose hair and weight. The teachers are saying he may or may not complete his HSC exams this year. He'll only be coming to school whenever he feels like it. Some of the younger kids in school who don't know about his condi-tion keep giving him awkward stares – he looks so out of place and we can tell he is uncomfortable.

My two mates and I are thinking of doing something special for him. We're thinking of shaving our heads (so he won't stand out so much) and in the process, raising funds for research into Hodgkin's lym-phoma. What do you think dad?"

My first emotional response was quite frankly, one of sheer relief. Re-lief that I had not opened my big mouth and stuck that foot in! The next thing I felt was a deep sense of pride. You know that moment in your child's life when they transition from the "me" to "we" phase — a phase we all go through in our journey towards independence and interdependence? For me, that was *the golden* moment for Aaron. I said to him, "Son, if that's why you want to do what you want to do, of course you have our blessing. I couldn't be prouder of you. Mum and I chose to send you to that school because of its reputation of living up to its' motto "Ad Majora Natus" (In Latin, it means "Men for others. Born for greater things.") You exemplify that. In fact, let us know what we can do to help."

He replied, "Dad, I could do with some advice. My friends and I ap-proached our Year 12 coordinator about this and we said, "Sir, we're thinking of helping Johnny by shaving our heads." Without even hearing us out, he immediately blurted, "You guys are already seniors in this school. You should know the rules. I can't believe you're even thinking of this!" Geez dad. What about Ad Majora Natus? What should we do?"

I empathised with his frustration and then calmly asked him how committed he was towards achieving his goal. Hearing his determination to see it through, I suggested that he first decide not to give up and instead to use this as an opportunity to learn how he could influence more effectively. I told him that he was born to be a game-changer and that in life, the ability to influence upwards was such an important skill to have. I shared with him that whenever people were reactive, they were usually doing this under duress (and the effect of cortisol). I suggested that his teacher simply meant to say that whilst he applauded their wonderful gesture of helping a mate, he was concerned about the negative precedence this might set for the rest of the kids and the reputational damage it might cause the school. Members of the public might see them walking around with shaved heads without understanding the context.

I suggested that he find a suitable time to speak to his teacher again, to thank him for hearing them out previously, and to express their empathy of how he might be concerned about their suggestion. Then see if he would be open to hearing some ideas they had on how they may be able to help Johnny without affecting the school's integrity. Perhaps they could offer to step up to the podium during the next school assembly and suggest to the Year 12 cohort to make it a Year 12 project

— for everyone to shave their heads. In the process, they could ask for donations for research into Hodgkin's Lymphoma. They could offer to draft a message to all parents explaining what they were looking to do and to enlist their understanding and support.

I could tell from his silent nods and eye contact that Aaron had been taking all this in. When I finished, he simply said, "Hmmm. This could work. Thanks dad."

That was the end of our conversation. Now consider this. What do you think the outcome would have been? Would the trust and relationship between my son and I have strengthened as a result of the conversation we had, how we both felt during the conversation and the tone that was used? I'd like to think so! As a result of acting calmly and rationally, would Aaron be even more willing to come to me to seek my ideas in future? Probably. Those were the two most important outcomes I wanted. There was a third outcome — convincing him to not go ahead with his plan without the permission of his teacher — but whether or not I achieved this outcome wasn't in my control.

Now imagine if I had utilised these skills while responding to Keith's news that fateful morning when he told me of his decision to restructure my organisation. When instead of interpreting his call as a threat and going into fear and "freeze" mode, I calmly changed the way I felt, and said, "Tell me more". How might that have influenced my relationship with my manager and how I subsequently dealt with that situation? How might the next two years have been?

All I know is that one week later, Aaron came home with a shaven head. We didn't discuss it. I've often reminded my children that I was there to offer them advice when they wanted it but that they were to own their decisions (and any consequences) and I would respect their decisions, no matter what. I simply hoped that he hadn't gotten himself into trouble at school.

About six months later, my wife and I were to learn what really happened. We attended a function organised by the school called the Valete dinner. It was an annual tradition, a dinner attended by all Year 12 students with their parents. It was organised by the school as their way of congratulating and saying farewell to this cohort. That evening, we got to share a meal with our son, his friends and their parents with a meal served by the Year 11 parents. While we were enjoying our meal, they showed a slideshow of the cohort's special moments in school. There was hardly a dry eye in the audience when they showed a picture of the Year 12 cohort standing proud, all with shaven heads.

Consider the impact this might have had on Johnny and his family. What about this band of brothers – would this have created a lasting bond between them? And wasn't this a powerful way of the school communicating to its students the true meaning of "Ad Majora Natus"?

I actually don't know what transpired after my discussion with my son. All I know is that applying the following four gifts made all the difference to the outcome I achieved in our conversation:

- **Self-awareness** — the ability to read my emotions and know that I was experiencing fear, and that reacting in times of fear wasn't constructive. Knowing that it wasn't the change or situation that was causing me to feel fear, but my perception that the change or situation was a threat. Knowing in advance what was most important to me, taking the long-term perspective in view. And making a key outcome from every interaction I have with others around me that a) the relationship and rapport grows deeper, and b) the other person feels even better about him or herself after the interaction.

- **Imagination** — visualising the ideal outcomes I wanted to achieve from the situation in advance and appreciating the consequences of my choice of action.

- **Conscience** — really testing my assumptions about my son's request and reminding myself of all that was great about my son.

- **Independent will** — choosing to overcome my subconscious habit of reacting by thinking "Why is this happening?" and instead responding calmly and positively by reflecting on "What's GREAT about this?" (turning fear into gratitude for the fact that I had a great relationship with a son who was not hesitant to come to me for my advice).

In summary, know that while our environment and our conditioned perceptions about that environment can affect how we feel, through the application of self-awareness and self-control we can actually choose how we respond.

Self-control is a result of applying these four unique gifts. [14]Stephen R Covey found that one of the key habits that distinguish highly effective people from others is that they're proactive. He says: "The key to being proactive (the opposite of reactive) is remembering that between stimulus and response there is a space. That space represents our choice — how we will choose to respond to any given situation, person, thought, or event. Imagine a pause button between stimulus and response — a button you can engage to pause and think about what is the principle-based response to your given situation. Listen to what your conscience tells you. Listen for what is wise and the principle-based thing to do, and then act.[21]"

The choices we make in these spaces determine our destiny. The extent to which we are able to exercise these four gifts of self-awareness, imagination, conscience and self-control in these microseconds and choose to respond rather than react, affects the quality of our life and relationships, our level of resilience, and how we respond to change.

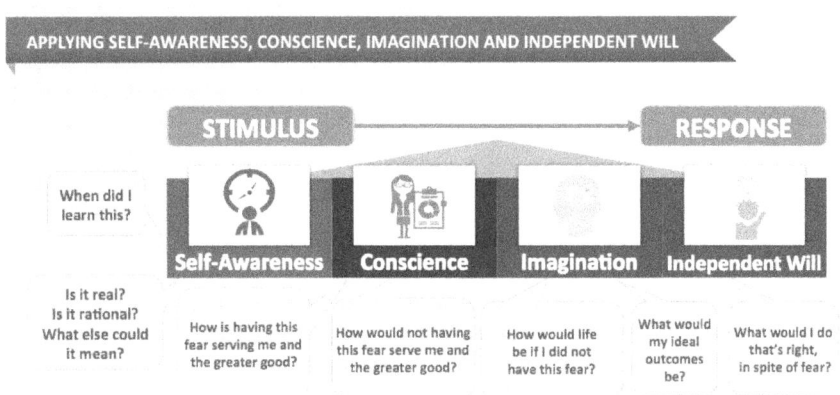

Figure 9 - Applying Self-Awareness, Imagination, Conscience and Independent Will

Similarly, when facing change, whenever we feel stressed and fearful, remember that it's not the change, but the disempowering meaning we're giving to the change (our perception that it's a threat) that's affecting the way we feel. Learn not to judge the event. You may have heard the saying, "Don't ASS-U-ME. It makes an ass out of you and me." Unless you knew everything that would transpire as a result of every event that would happen, why would you assume the worst? Instead, exercise your faith that everything happens for a positive reason.

Rather than react with fear, practise self-control through the habit of pressing the PAUSE button and then turn your emotional state from fear to states such as calm, confidence, and love to help you deal with such situations much more positively.

CHAPTER 5

How Resilient People Move

Your emotional state is affected by the way you move, breathe, hold your body, your level of rest, hydration and diet

Move and breathe the way you wish to feel

Make working out regularly part of your daily rituals

Smile and be a hugger!

Get sufficient and good quality sleep and rest

Ensure your diet is rich with water-based foods and quality nutritional supplements

"*Everything is energy and that is all there is to it. Match the frequency of the reality you want and you cannot help but get that reality. It can be no other way. This is not philosophy. This is physics*"

— *Albert Einstein*

Act the way you want to feel

In the previous chapter, we made the point that one of the key traits of winners is their ability to exercise self-control and manage their emotional state. In simple terms, this means the ability to choose to press the *pause/breathe/reflect* button whenever they're feeling threatened rather than react and fall victim to the negativity bias and the amygdala hijack.

Those microseconds between the event and our response allow us to take stock of our emotions and then to choose a more empowering emotional state before responding. The question then is — *how* can we create the new state we expect?

One of the best pieces of advice I ever got was to "Act the way you want to feel."

Our emotional state and moods are affected by many factors, including our social and physical environment, diet, exercise, and daily sleep patterns. These same factors affect the hormones that regulate our brain's response system. [1]Changes in our level of hormones influence our neurotransmitters (such as dopamine and serotonin), which, in turn, affect our emotional state. Our emotional state therefore is inextricably linked to our hormones. [2]Cortisol (also known as the stress hormone) induces states of stress and fear, while dopamine (the pleasure or desire hormone), serotonin (the "feel-good" hormone), oxytocin and endorphins (think "runner's high") bring about feelings of pleasure and desire. [3]We can actually regulate these hormones and thus our emotional state by being aware of and altering the way we move, our posture, the way we breathe, how we sleep, and what we eat.

Movement

We are creatures of habit. Even the way we *move* is habitual. I remember during my period of great uncertainty at IBM, I used to walk in a slow, ponderous manner. What I wasn't aware of at the time was that moving this way was putting me in a low-energy state. **If you want to change the way you feel, simply *move* the way you want to feel.**

Want to feel energised? Think about how an energised person walks or moves and start moving that way.

Activity

Stand up, find a quiet spot and just move in a vigorous, energetic way for about 30 seconds. Exaggerate that movement to take your energy level up to a level 10. How does that make you feel? See how quickly you can change your state?

Want to feel more confident? Think about how a confident person moves — straight back, strong, long and quick strides with your hands pumping at your side. Go ahead and move that way right now. How does that make you feel?

Want to feel happy? Think about how a happy person moves. Start moving that way.

The hormones in our blood stream affect our emotions. Physical activity is a powerful way of triggering endorphins and serotonin, which in turn positively alter the way we feel.

Learning that I could create any emotional state I wanted simply by being conscious of and altering the way I move, was incredibly empowering.

The environment (events, situations external to us, other people's moods) can affect how we feel, however, they do not *determine* the way we feel. Knowing that I could choose my emotional state in any situation was incredibly liberating.

I decided then and there to consciously develop the habit of moving like a person who exuded courage, faith, fun, and love.

I remember learning about this technology over a weekend and then choosing to immediately put that into practise. That very Monday, I strode into my office with a big grin on my face and a strong, confident stride. I assembled my team into an impromptu briefing and said, "For the last two years, I have come to the office each day looking like the world was about to end. I have been your absent leader. I have let you down. I'll never be able to wind back the clock but if you'll allow me to, I intend to fully make up for that. Over the weekend, I learned that it's not what happens to us in life, it's what we do that matters. I've learned that the trick to living a successful and fulfilling life is to simply decide to make each and every day the most extraordinary day we can, to utilise our skills to make a difference and to have fun in the process. I choose to be immeasurably happier and more positive in everything I do. Please be patient with me as I may fall back to my old ways every now and then. But hold me accountable to this. You and I deserve nothing less."

When I got home that evening, instead of walking in like a zombie, I paused at my porch, took a few deep breaths and asked myself, "What would make my evening the most extraordinary experience for my family and me?" I imagined everyone's happy and enthusiastic faces at the dinner table sharing the events of our day and then, feeling determined, grateful and happy about the opportunity to make it happen, I opened the door and strode in with a huge smile on my face and a bright, cheery "I'm home! How's everyone's day been?"

These habits have made a huge difference to my experience of life and my relationship with others around me.

Breathing

Your body uses oxygen to create energy so managing the way we breathe is essential for optimum health. The way we breathe affects the way we feel, which affects our actions and outcomes. We tend to take sips of a breath and hold it when we're anxious, which can have a ripple effect through our system. One bad habit, like shallow breathing, triggers another. [4]Studies have shown that breathing incorrectly adversely impacts our digestive system, leads to hormonal imbalance and makes us more susceptible to lower back pain. Just think of high altitude mountain climbing — a lack of oxygen contributes to a whole host of nasty symptoms. Breathing properly, on the other hand, relaxes us, helps us keep the mind open, and enables us to think more clearly about what we want to do and why we're doing something. It improves our digestive system, improves balance, and gives us the best posture.

Just as our emotional state affects the way we breathe, the opposite is also true. During times of uncertainty, feeling calm and confident will help us think more clearly and make more rational decisions. To create such states, simply breathe like a person who's feeling that way.

Whenever I'm feeling anxious, taking a pause to draw in a few, deep "belly breaths" can instantly transport me into an oasis of calm. If I wish to make light of a situation, laughing out loud can also change the way I breathe and my emotional state in an instant. And if I choose to be confident, breathing like I do when I'm feeling self-assured quickly brings about that state.

This exercise is one I took on when I learned about the power of breath to create a positive state change. I recommend you do it at least twice a day (once in the morning and once in the evening). When you're at work, take a short break every 60 to 90 minutes and make time to do a set of 10 deep belly breaths.

* Relax your breathing mechanisms.

Stand up and plant your feet firmly on the floor, hip-width apart. Relax your shoulders. Soften your joints — ankles, knees, and hips. At the same time, feel your spine straighten up through your crown to the ceiling, so that you feel loose but have height. Keep your head straight but allow it to bob about slightly on the atlas joint (the pivot which makes it possible for you to nod).

* Breathe the right way for 10 repeats.

Place both hands, one on top of the other, over your stomach (using the belly button as the central point). Breathe in and feel your stomach expand; breathe out and push the stomach gently back in with it. We tend to "breathe backwards (hunching our shoulders and sucking our stomachs in when we take a deep breath); this exercise makes us aware of the correct way to breathe.

* Feel yourself expand as you breathe.

1. Draw a deep breath strongly for four counts.
2. Hold your breath for 12 counts – this allows time for the oxygen to permeate through the cells and collect toxins that could impair its optimal functioning (such toxins may have come

from a myriad of sources including diet, stress, or from simply the air that we breathe).

3. Breathe out for eight counts to allow the system to fully expel the toxins.

You'll find that at the end of five minutes you feel totally refreshed and re-energised. Through this ritual, you'll put yourself in a state of calm and will be totally present and in the moment. This is a great state to be in when dealing with stressful situations.

Posture and muscle tension

Another aspect of our physiology that affects our brain chemicals and how we feel is the way we hold our bodies — our posture, body and muscle tension. What you convey through your body (your body language or non-verbals) affects not just others around you, but also affects you!

Studies on embodied cognition show that changes to bodily movements, such as facial displays, can affect emotional states. For example, unobtrusive contraction of the "smile muscle" increases enjoyment (Strack, Martin, Stepper, 1988)[5], the head tilting upward induces pride (Stepper & Strack, 1993), and hunched postures (as opposed to upright postures) elicit more depressed feelings (Riskind & Gotay, 1982).

Every emotion has a unique pattern of breathing, posture and muscle tension associated with it. Think of someone who might be worried. What is their breathing like? Deep or shallow? Shallow right? What about their posture? Straight backed or slumped? Yes, you're right.

Slumped. What about the muscle tension around the shoulder region? And around their face?

What about someone who's happy? Deep, relaxed breathing, wide-open chest structure, big smile on their face.

Just changing your posture and releasing the muscle tension around your face, neck, shoulders and chest will change the way you feel.

Everyone talks about the importance of "body language", but few people understand how much of an impact it actually has — not just in the way others perceive us, but in terms of how *we* actually perform.

Harvard Business School professor and researcher Amy Cuddy's TED talk titled "Your Body Language shapes who you are[6]" is one of the most popular TED talks of all time. Certain "power poses" don't just change how others perceive you, Professor Cuddy says. They immediately change your body chemistry. She speaks specifically about "power posing" - standing in a posture of confidence (e.g. feet wide, hands on hips, body upright, confident facial expression — the "Wonder Woman" pose), even when we don't feel confident – can affect testosterone and cortisol levels in the brain, and thus our performance. Times of uncertainty can induce states of helplessness. People who *feel* powerful have higher rates of testosterone and lower states of cortisol.

Her research[6] showed that when people adopted a power pose for just two minutes, their levels of testosterone increased by 20% whilst their cortisol levels dropped by 10%. On the other hand, people who adopted "low power poses" (e.g. folding up, making oneself small) experienced a 25% reduction in testosterone levels and a 15% increase in cortisol!

Figure 10 - High versus low power pose

One that I do often is to stand strong, put a huge smile on my face, take in a deep breath, look up at the ceiling, squeeze my fists like I do when I'm feeling confident and determined, pump my hands in the air and go "Yes!"

Doing this power pose in combination with a positive affirmation creates an instantaneous state change that makes me feel ready to rumble and move forward in the most positive state.

During my challenging period, I'd wake up most mornings to the sound of the alarm, feeling totally exhausted. After I pressed the snooze button several times, the dread of getting into work late and stressed would get the better of the comfort of the doona. I'd drag myself out of bed and walk like a zombie to the bathroom.

These days, I have a very different ritual. After enjoying a minute's reflection on "what's great about my life right now" (we'll talk about this later in this book) and asking, "what's going to make today extraordinary?" I get out of bed, do my power pose and stride purposefully towards the bathroom. This simple exercise puts me in the most empowered state, ready and excited about what lies ahead!

Smile

> *"Sometimes your joy is the source of your smile, but sometimes your smile can be the source of your joy."* — *Thich Nhat Hanh*

I remember during those dark days when I'd trudge home from work, exhausted and stressed (often wearing a frown), and how being greeted by my wife's warm, loving smile would totally lift up my day. It made me feel like the most important person in the world and that everything was just fine.

We know that smiling greatly improves our mood and reduces stress. Even better, just like power posing, the act of smiling even when you don't feel like it offers you the same physiological and emotional benefits of a smile that's natural and spontaneous. Go ahead, I know you've been itching to do this for a while now so just put on that best grin you can muster and see how great it feels (why not see if you can hold it while you're reading this book?).

The act of putting a wide grin on your face activates the release of neuropeptides that fight off stress. Neuropeptides are tiny molecules that allow neurons to communicate. They facilitate messaging to the whole body when we're happy, sad, angry, depressed, or excited. The feel-good hormones dopamine, endorphins and serotonin are all released when a smile flashes across your face as well, and this not only relaxes your body, but it can lower your heart rate and blood pressure as well.

[7]Serotonin also acts as a natural pain reliever — 100% organically and without the negative side effects of synthetic concoctions! The serotonin release brought about by your smile serves as an anti-depressant/mood lifter. All these amazing benefits, and all for free. With just a little effort initially, and persistence as you consciously do this for a few days, you'll find that the pleasure or reward you receive then turns it into a habit. [7]Scientists and spiritual teachers alike agree that this simple act can transform you and the world around you. It's contagious, can make us more attractive to others, lifts our moods and the moods of those around us, and it can even lengthen our lives.

How a smile affects your brain

Most powerfully, a smile can change your brain. [8]In a 2009 study, scientists at Echnische Universitat in Munich, Germany used fMRI (functional MRI) imaging to measure brain activity in regions of emotional processing in the brain before and after injecting Botox to suppress smiling muscles. The findings showed that when you smile, your brain is aware of the activity and actually keeps track of it. The more you smile, the more effective you are at breaking the brain's natural tendency to think negatively. If you smile often enough, you end up re-wiring your brain to make positive patterns more often than it does negative ones.

Smiles strengthen relationships

You actually look better when you smile, and when you do, people treat you differently since you're viewed as attractive, reliable, relaxed and sincere. A study published in the journal Neuropsychologia[7] reported that seeing an active smiling face activates the orbitofrontal cortex - the region in your brain that processes sensory rewards. This suggests that when you view a smiling person, you actually feel rewarded.

It also explains the 2011 findings by researchers at the [7]Face Research Laboratory at the University of Aberdeen, Scotland. Subjects were asked to rate smiling and attractiveness. They found that both men and women were more attracted to images of people who made eye contact and smiled, compared to those who didn't. If you don't believe me, see how many looks you get when you walk outside with that smile you're wearing right now. (You're still smiling like I asked, right?)

In all seriousness, consider this. Imagine an organisation is going through change and there's a position that comes up with quite a few people going for it. Who would the managers pick? The person who comes in to work with a frown and projects negative energy, or the one who's always smiling and upbeat?

Smile and the whole world smiles back at you

Here's another benefit of smiling: Not only does it make you feel great, it makes others feel great as well. And when others feel great, their actions and happiness comes right back to you, creating a positive spiral of happiness. We've all heard that emotions are contagious right? You know when someone in a room yawns and it starts a ripple effect? It's the same with a smile. The part of your brain that's responsible for your facial muscles smiling when happy or mimicking another's smile resides in the cingulate cortex, an **unconscious** automatic response area.

In a Swedish study, subjects were shown pictures of several emotions; joy, anger, fear and surprise. When the picture of someone smiling was presented, the researchers asked the subjects to frown. Instead, they found that the facial expressions went directly to imitation of what the subjects saw. It took conscious effort to turn that smile upside down. So if you're smiling at someone, it's likely they can't help but smile back. If they don't, they're making a conscious effort not to.

Smiling can help you live longer

Aside from your mental state, smiling can also end up saving your life, as Sondra Barrett claims in her book "Secrets of Your Cells[8]".

The biochemist says that when you let go of tension - an outcome that can be achieved through smiling - your cells let go of their rigidness. According to Barrett's research, this could end up saving your life as there have been cases where cancer patients go into remission of cancer after letting go of a big stress factor.

"Our cells are more than just fortuitous arrangements of chemicals," she explains. "They are a community of trillions of sentient entities cooperating to create a sanctuary for the human soul."

Looking at the bigger picture, each time you smile at a person, their brain coaxes them to return the favour. You're creating a symbiotic relationship that allows both of you to release feel-good chemicals in your brain, activate reward centres, make you both more attractive and increase the chances of you both living longer, healthier lives.

Scientifically speaking, smiling more is a great thing for your life. Your career might even take a turn for the better as productivity increases, your attention span and cognitive abilities are improved, and you exude competence everywhere you go. With all of these benefits, who wouldn't want to start smiling more?

So here's a challenge for you. Starting today, begin smiling more. Every time you pass someone, establish eye contact and just flash those pearly whites. Send positive feelings of love and appreciation that come from the deepest part of your soul. See what sort of response you get. Don't be disheartened if you don't get one back, but I think you'll find that more often than not, you will. My personal experience found that in most Western societies, around six to seven out of 10 will respond really positively and your action will cause them to smile at you. In Asia, this drops down to around three to four. Your action might solicit a surprised look from some, most of whom after the initial surprise, will smile warmly at you in a show of gratitude. Do note that cultural sensitivity is important. In certain cultures, it can be considered improper for men to do this to women they don't know.

Learning and turning smiling into a habit has made a significant difference to my life. In fact, I make it part of my daily mission to bring a smile to the face of people I meet. My family have benefitted and they're all great smilers - yes, even our dog Piper! When we arrive home each day, being greeted by her loving smile and the smiles and hugs of my family members, this feels amazing.

Work Out!

From a medium to long-term perspective, having a regular exercise regimen that combines both cardiovascular and strength building exercises, is one of the most constructive habits you can form not only to manage your stress levels but to regularly put yourself in your most empowering emotional state. [9]Exercise plays a key role in the function of our hormones – particularly those contributing to the way we look (muscle building, fat cell shrinkage), and feel (mood and stress levels). Working out releases endorphins, sometimes referred to as "runner's high"[10]. Endorphins produce a sense of happiness and positive well-being[11].

From my teenage years to my early thirties, I regularly exercised. Being a passionate badminton player who competed in tournaments;

workouts were almost a daily routine. When I stopped playing regularly, either due to injuries or just through allowing the busyness of work and the added time pressures to get to me, my consistency dropped off significantly. At a time when stress levels were the highest and I probably needed it most, my ritual of social badminton dwindled down to once or twice a week. Because playing badminton was often a three to four hour commitment each time, during the time when I had a very heavy work schedule, it was often replaced by the occasional 20-minute jog around the neighbourhood whenever I felt particularly lethargic. I never really looked at exercise and physical movement as a means to manage my energy levels or create the most empowering emotional state I needed. The more stressed I got, the more tired I felt. I must admit to periods where the comfort of the couch overrode any desire for physical exercise. When I learned about the link between our emotional state, our performance, and our experience of life, I was determined to change this.

The first decision I made was to live an extraordinary life. I visualised the state of health, vitality and energy I wanted at age 80. I didn't just want to live a long life, but one where I could really have the energy and buzz to do everything I wanted and to enjoy it to the fullest. I didn't want to get to 80 and worry about remembering the names of people around me — I wanted to be running around with my grandkids and even great grandkids, be able to toss the young ones up in the sky and be an inspiration to them, about what it was like to live to the full, no matter how old one was.

I wanted to continue to see and explore the full beauty of the world before my time was up and that included being able to swim, snorkel, trek and generally do everything a strong, able-bodied 30-year-old ought to be at a grand old age. I wanted to be able to continue to run workshops for large groups of people and be an inspiration to them just by the boundless energy I would show up with and my zest for life. After getting clear with my vision for my physiology, I realised that I needed to lift my game to not only create the most empowering and energising states for me each and every day, but to also give myself the best chance of being in such a peak state when I was well into my 80s, 90s and 100s. I saw lots of people around me who, when they got to retirement age in their late 50s and 60s, began to lose the sparkle in their eyes and spend much of their time and money trying to recover the health and energy that they'd neglected for so many years.

And so just before I turned 40 and with that long-term vision in mind, I decided to lift my game. I first set my sights on running a marathon. This had long been a "bucket list" item for me. I'd never been a runner, in fact, running was something I "had to" do in order to compete in badminton.

And so, when I did the occasional jogging thing, I found it hard to maintain any form of enthusiasm for it because I didn't have a specific target. I've found that a specific target like "completing a marathon by this date" gives me a lot more power and enthusiasm for the training I must do to get there than one that says "get fit". Setting a huge goal like a marathon would mean I absolutely had to get a regular routine in place. After I'd completed my marathon, I set another goal, which was to complete a 100 km trek in an annual event run by Oxfam to raise funds for those in need. The point I'm making is this:

- How you perform during times of change is directly related to the energy levels and emotional state you're able to maintain during that period.

- Achieving the most extraordinary outcomes starts with creating rituals that will help you create the most extraordinary emotional state.

- The easiest way to change the way you feel is to alter and balance your inner chemistry.

- A constructive, powerful way to do this and also to give you some "me" time is to develop a habit of regular exercise.

- To sustain this habit, firstly create a long-term vision for what you'd like your energy levels to be 10–20 years from now. Imagine and emotionalise the benefits of being in that peak state of vitality. Who could you positively impact and in what way? How would that make you feel?

- Having done that, create a short-term SMART goal. One that's Specific, Measurable, Actionable, Realistic and Time bound. E.g. "To lose 20 kgs by 25 December 2018" or "To complete the City to Surf event in Sydney 2018 within 90 minutes" is much more effective than "To get fit". And then work with a coach or do some research to put together a training plan to make that work.

- Ideally, you will want to develop a regimen that includes cardiovascular and strength building exercises. If you haven't exercised for a while or don't have a regular routine, start with small steps e.g. three 20-minute sessions either on a stationary bike, treadmill or even a brisk walk.

- Find a way to reward yourself with something pleasurable right after you've completed the workout. Any activity that our sub-conscious mind associates pleasure with tends to be more sustainable than one we associate with pain. This could be watching your favourite program, dancing to your favourite song, or even indulging in a small piece of your favourite chocolate. The key is to persist with this habit until it becomes fun.

Today, working out regularly (four to five times a week on an average of 45 minutes per session) has become part of my weekly routine. It's something I really enjoy and I feel exceptionally great after every workout. Having kept this routine for close to 15 years now, I'm feeling stronger and energised. My energy levels allow me to sustain a demanding work and travel schedule and importantly, to enjoy every moment of every day. It has also contributed significantly to my stress management and most importantly, made me a much happier person.

Sleep

I'm sure you've read that the amount and quality of sleep we get has a direct impact on our moods. Being a frequent traveller who has to deal with the effects of jet lag and the need to maintain very high levels of energy for my workshops, I am acutely aware of the impact sleep has on my moods and performance levels.

[12]Everyone needs a different amount of sleep, but in general, research shows that seven to eight hours is ideal. One of the most practical habits you can develop to help yourself be even more resilient and positive is to ensure you get enough sleep. There are a ton of books out there about how to get a great night's sleep, and rather than pretend to be an expert on this topic, I'll highlight some of the key tips that have helped me most:

- Research on REM sleep (the deepest most restful sleep we can have) and the rhythmic cycles our body goes through has shown that sleeping and waking earlier (around 10 pm would be ideal but no later than 11 pm ideally) is best.

- Establish a little routine where you cut down on the use of technology at least an hour or two before bedtime.

- A warm drink, quiet music or dimming the light in the room during this pre-sleep period is helpful.

- Do your best to have a meal that's not too heavy over dinner and finish that meal at least three to four hours before bedtime (this minimises the amount of energy your body is taking to digest food and thus gives the body an optimal opportunity to rest and recreate).

Mindfulness and Meditation

For years, I'd been told about the benefits of Mindfulness and Mindfulness Meditation to help manage my tendency to be reactive. And yet, I must admit that the mere thought of creating "downtime" to sit cross-legged (which I find most uncomfortable, partly due to an arthritic knee that's been abused through years of playing badminton and running) and think of nothing had not been particularly appealing!

The term "mindfulness" is defined as the moment-to-moment awareness of one's experience without judgment. Whilst I have personally experienced first-hand or witnessed people close to me (like my mum) benefit from practises that cultivate mindfulness such as yoga, tai chi and qigong, the practise I'd like to specifically encourage you to consider incorporating into your ritual for developing resilience is mindfulness meditation.

Mindfulness meditation is a self-regulation practise that focuses on training one's attention and awareness in order to bring mental processes under greater voluntary control and thereby foster general mental well-being and development and specific capacities such as calmness, clarity and concentration (Walsh & Shapiro, 2006). The research extolling the benefits of mindfulness is compelling and includes the following:

- **Reduced rumination.** In 2008, Chambers et al. asked 20 novice meditators to participate in a 10-day intensive mindfulness meditation retreat. After the retreat, the meditation group reported a higher level of mindfulness, experienced fewer depressive symptoms and were less likely to ruminate which means to focus on the symptoms, possible causes and consequences in times of distress rather than solutions.

- **Stress reduction.** In 2010, Farb et al found through research involving participants watching sad films and using fMRI to scan neural activity, that those who practised mindfulness meditation experienced significantly less anxiety, depression and somatic distress.

- **Focus.** In 2009, Moore and Malinowski found that mindfulness meditation strengthened one's ability to focus attention and suppress distracting information.

- **Less emotional reactivity.** In a study of people who had anywhere from one month to 29 years of mindfulness meditation practice, researchers found that mindfulness meditation practice helped people disengage from emotionally upsetting pictures. It enabled them to focus better on a cognitive task as compared with people who saw the pictures but did not meditate (Ortner et al., 2007).

The anecdotal evidence is pretty compelling too. Tim Ferriss[13] (author of the New York Times and Wall Street Journal best-sellers "The Four-Hour Workweek", "The Four-Hour Body" and "The Four-Hour Chef) whose work and podcast (called "The Tim Ferriss Show") I love, has interviewed more than 200 world-class performers for his show since 2014. His guests have ranged from super celebrities (Jamie Foxx, Arnold Schwarzenegger, etc.) and athletes (icons of powerlifting, gymnastics, surfing, etc.) to legendary Special Operations commanders. What he found is that of all the routines and habits practised by his guests, the most common one was some form of daily meditation or mindfulness practice. More than 80% of the world-class performers he interviewed shared this trait. This applies to everyone from Arnold Schwarzenegger to Justin Boreta of The Glitch Mob, and from elite athletes like Amelia Boone to writers like Maria Popova. Their experience was that mindfulness meditation is a "meta-skill" that improves everything else. Starting each day with practising focus when it *didn't* matter (sitting on a couch for 10 minutes) helped them focus better later when it *did* matter (negotiating a deal, conversing with a loved one, maximising a deadlift, writing a best-seller, etc.). Given my commitment to model those whose results I want to have, late last year I decided to seriously give it a go.

For me, being mindful is simply about being fully present to the moment. It could mean that as I'm typing this, instead of simply feeling the pressure to complete this segment so I can send it off to my editor, Stacey, I can just take a few seconds to appreciate that I'm sitting comfortably on an extra leg-room seat and that my flight is really smooth. I can appreciate the general silence of the cabin I'm in, notice the soothing hum of the engines, the tenseness of my butt-cheeks (and my immediate efforts to relax them) and to focus on my breathing and posture. I could close my eyes for just a moment and focus on "scanning" my body from my temple to my toes, feeling and releasing any tensions that I may be experiencing and at the same time, keeping my focus on my breathing. Whenever I observe a thought emerging to disrupt my focus, I gently let the thought go and just get back to focussing on my breathing and what is known as the "space between our thoughts". As a thought comes up, I just gently get back to focussing on the space. In simple terms, this is what mindfulness meditation is all about.

Whilst I intellectually understood the benefits of mindful meditation, it actually took me a few years to get from a "going-on-it-for-a-few-days-and-then-losing-interest" mode to today when it's become an almost daily and at times twice daily ritual for me that I really look forward to.

I'm not sure about you but I've found that when I'm feeling pressured and stressed, my mind tends to race a million miles per hour. I'm either worrying about whether or not what I did yesterday was good enough, or thinking of how I might have done it better, or considering what I need to do tomorrow. I find it too easy to lose sight of just treasuring the present moment.

During times of change and when we're stressed, particularly for those of us who are "task-oriented", we can allow our thoughts to dictate our emotions, which in turn drives our behaviours and outcomes. By being cognisant of this and incorporating disciplined moments of mindful meditation and other moments, where we just pull back and simply observe our thoughts without reacting to them, we can bring about immediate changes to our emotional state. This takes us to a place of calm, peace and bliss - states that empower us to act more positively and constructively.

By making this a regular practice, you'll find that it gets easier and easier over time, and you'll find ever-growing precious moments of tranquillity.

Action Plan

If you'd like to consider mindful meditation but don't know where to start, I have found it useful to have a guide. If you Google meditation, you'll find a wide (and if you're like me, confusing array of different schools and styles of meditation. By all means research them, check out reviews about them and if you find a particular method that resonates with you, visit a place that's convenient to you that offers "free" or "try-before-you-buy" classes. I'm still a relative newbie to this, so I can't really offer you decent advice on the relative merits of each style or school of thought. Decide to visit them, and if what you learn from the first class makes sense, commit to sticking it out for at least 10 days in a row. You may find initially that you do not experience many radical benefits or change — much like you might if it's the first time to a gym, apart from some discomfort or "pain". Decide to see through this initial "seed planting" phase where you may not see the shoots of your labour. After 10 days of disciplined application, you can then decide if the benefits you are starting to experience are worth you making it a regular ritual. I've personally found it to be incredibly enriching and helpful in dealing positively with challenge and stress.

For me, rather than get to a class, I meditate with the help of an app called Headspace, with a wonderful voice guiding me through 10 min-utes of meditation each day (I intend to take this to 20 minutes at least once a day in due course). I started with the free Take10 challenge (10 minutes a day for 10 consecutive days), and have since been hooked on this ritual. I find it works great first thing in the morning after I've risen and brushed my teeth and written in my Gratitude Log. I do it seated comfortably on my favourite seat in my home – my electric leather recliner (one of the few luxuries I've indulged in and am ever so glad I did) – and with my feet just resting on the foot-rest.

Whenever I've done it in the evening before dinner, it feels like I've started the day anew. It has helped me considerably in creating the energy and focus I choose to put into constructive endeavours like writing this book.

So if you prefer, go ahead and download the App called Headspace and start your Take10 challenge today. You'll be glad you did this!

Diet and Hydration

As much as 60% of our body weight is made up of water[14]. The brain and heart are composed of **73%** water, and the lungs about 83%[14].

Every system in your body depends on water. For instance, water is needed by the brain to manufacture hormones and neurotransmitters, form saliva for digestion. Water allows our body's cells to grow, reproduce and survive, regulate our body temperature, flush out body waste, help deliver oxygen all over the body and convert food to the components needed for survival.

Stress, exhaustion and lethargy are often just symptoms of dehydration[15].

Take note of how you're feeling right now. What's your level of energy? Now pour yourself a glass of water and drink its entire contents right away. How does that make you feel? More energised?

During times of stress and change, your autoimmune system is particularly vulnerable. Keeping yourself well hydrated and giving your body the right fuels will help you be at your peak physiological state.

Both my mum, Rose and my mother-in-law, Lily were diagnosed of autoimmune disorders in their early 50s. Rose with a condition called Sjogren's syndrome and Lily with schleroderma. Both spent years working on managing their pain levels. One day about 15 years ago, I worked with a coach who had me reflect on the following question: "If you were given but six months to live, what would you do with the rest of your life?" One of the goals I set was to find a way to help my mum and mother-in-law cope better with this debilitating condition.

Through research, I learned that the field of medicinal science is gener-ally focussed on treating, not preventing illnesses. Unfortunately, there remains today no cure for conditions like Sjogren's syndrome and sch-leroderma. At the most basic level, all we're made up of is trillions of cells, each like a power generator giving us life! Our cells regenerate all the time and three of the most critical fuels it needs to stay vital are oxygen, nutrients and healthy thoughts. Throughout the early 20th century, most illness-related deaths were caused by conditions such as typhoid, tuberculosis, even the common flu – all typically caused by bacteria. Dramatic improvements in medicinal science in the areas of detection, immunisation, surgery and the treatment of diseases caused by bacteria, means life expectancies are longer than ever.

[16]Today, the major illness-related diseases that are killing us are can-cer, heart disease, stroke, diabetes, Alzheimer's, autoimmune disorders (such as schleroderma, rheumatoid arthritis, lupus and Sjogren's syn-drome) and osteoporosis. [17]These diseases are caused by degeneration of the human cell and oxidative stress, which is ultimately largely a result of our lifestyle. Such lifestyle factors include:

- High stress levels and poor time management has resulted in less time for physical activity and exercise.

- Shallow breathing habits deprive our cells of the oxygen it needs.

- Growing consumption of highly processed foods with low nutrient levels is starving our cells of the vital nutrients it craves.

- Toxins ingested from polluted air and foods laden with pesticides elevate oxidative stress which causes our cells to degenerate.

- Debilitating negative thinking habits results in even more stress.

Here are some simple tips and strategies I've personally applied to this area of my life to keep myself in good shape and to supply the high levels of energy I need to be at my very best physically and mentally every day.

Hydrate yourself well. You've probably heard the saying "drink eight x 8-ounce glasses of filtered water a day". That's about 1.9 litres. Whist this is a good rule of thumb to follow, know that you will need to vary this depending on factors like exercise, illness, pregnancy, breastfeeding, weather conditions and more. In general, what I've learned is that most people under-estimate the amount of water consumption they need. To make up for this, I would generally err and consciously consume more than I felt I needed until this became a habit. For years, I used to have a massive headache at the end of every workshop I ran. I used to put this down to the stress of having to think on my feet at all times and maintain a high level of concentration and energy. Ever since I've carried a large container of water with me every day, consuming around 600mls of water every 1.5 hours, my post-workshop migraines have dramatically been reduced. Your fluid intake is probably fine if you drink enough fluid that you rarely feel thirsty and your urine is colourless or light yellow.

Increase your consumption of water-rich foods. If you're a huge meat eater, cut down on it and increase your portion of fruits and veggies. As the saying goes, "an apple a day keeps the doctor away". Raw vegetables and fruits are better than cooked, and steamed is better than fried. All in moderation. Not only do much of the nutrients and minerals that our cells need to thrive ultimately come from the ground, but fruits and veggies are easier for your body to digest — which means more energy for the other stuff.

Include food that's rich with omega-3 fatty acids.[18]Fish is one of the healthiest foods on the planet. It's loaded with important nutrients, such as protein and vitamin D. Fish is also the world's best source of omega-3 fatty acids, which are incredibly important for your body and brain. Nuts are also a great source of protein.

Eat in moderation. In general, don't consume more calories than you put out if you're wanting to maintain a healthy waistline. Our metabolic rate slows down as we age which means the system is not able to process and burn calories as efficiently as it used to. Not only does a healthy waistline help you feel better about yourself, it puts less strain on your structure.

Supplement your diet with high-quality nutritional supplements. This is an area that is highly controversial with many medical practitioners and some research claiming that most vitamins and supplements are nothing more than "expensive urine". I encourage you to do your own research. The reality is that the foods we consume today are not half as nutritious as the ones our forefathers readily had access to. For example, in 1948, a bowl of spinach contained about 150 milligrams of iron. But today that same bowl of spinach contains only about two milligrams![19]

Modern farming techniques (which do not give land the time to regenerate its nutrients), and the need for fruits and veggies to be transported large distances and with long shelf lives, means they are often reaped prematurely (most of the nutrients contained in raw foods from the ground are only produced close to ripening). This has resulted in the raw produce looking great but being starved of nutrients. Personally, I've researched and have a lot of trust in products from Usana Health Sciences. They've benefitted members of my family significantly in our health, vitality and energy levels. My mum in particular is a tremendous testimonial to the power of being proactive about prevention and energy management through a good supplemented diet, a regular workout regimen, and an attitude of grace, gratitude, and optimism.

During times of stress and anxiety, it's tempting to take short cuts with our diet. But this is the time that you need to manage your energy and vitality levels most. Put yourself in a peak physiological state by incorporating some of these habits into your lifestyle.

We may not have control over many of the changes that occur around us, but what we regularly consume is certainly an area of our life we have total control over.

Be a hugger

During times of change, you will want to make decisions calmly and rationally, not under conditions of high cortisol-fuelled, survival-driven stress. [20]Another hormone that stimulates growth and supports proactive, rational decision-making is oxytocin, also known as the "cuddle hormone". Oxytocin is a neuropeptide and promotes feelings of devotion, trust and bonding. A powerful, simple way to stimulate greater levels of oxytocin and at the same time reduce our levels of cortisol is to develop the habit of meaningful hugging or touch (with someone who appreciates that from you of course!).

For some years now, social scientists have validated that supportive touch reduces stress[21]. In a study[21] conducted by the Touch Research Institute at the University of Miami in Florida, subjects were asked to do something stressful, like public speaking or taking a timed math test. The subjects' partners were also part of the experiment and were asked to hug or hold their partner's hands when the researchers told them to. They found that people who performed these tasks while they were being hugged or while holding hands with their partners had lower blood pressure and a lower heart rate, suggesting that they were less stressed.

Consider the following other examples of the benefits of supportive touch:

If a teacher touches a student on the back or arm, that student is more likely to participate in class. The more that athletes high-five or hug their teammates, the better their game. A touch can make patients like their doctors more. If you touch a bus driver, he's more likely to let you on for free.

So, to increase your resilience, learn the habit of connecting more with others who care about you. Growing up in my very traditional and conservative family, I wasn't encouraged to be outwardly expressive. Other than the day I left Malaysia for Australia, I can't remember being hugged by members of my family.

When I learned that this was simply a powerful, empowering habit to develop, I began putting this into practise with my family and we're now a family of huggers. My sons are now 21 and 24 — we hug! Why not use everything great our Creator has given us to create the most empowering emotional states for ourselves and those around us?

Conclusion

In short, our physiology – the way we move, breathe, hold our bodies, and what we consume and how we connect with others, affects our emotional state. The easiest way to change the way you feel is to simply act the way you wish to feel. To feel powerful, confident, courageous, calm, happy, loving, grateful and inspired, choose to move, stand, breathe and smile like someone who feels empowered, confident, happy and inspired. Know also that what you feed your body affects the way you feel. Stay well hydrated and consume foods that are rich in vitamins and water content. This is the simplest and often the quickest, most constructive way to strengthen your resilience and put yourself in the most empowered states, regardless of the situation you are in.

Making the change

Learning what I've shared with you through this chapter was profound and incredibly empowering for me. The realisation that my environment could affect the way I felt, but did not *decide* the way I felt was a massive "ah ha" moment for me. I understood that while the change may not entirely have been of my choosing, how I had responded to it had totally been my decision. When everything else is taken away from you, know that there is one thing no one can ever take away from you – **your power to choose your response**. After all, I could change the way I felt simply by throwing my hands up in the air, smiling from the deepest part of my being, and going "YES!!!!" **I could feel how I wanted to feel in any situation in a heartbeat!**

The techniques were simple, but not easy, not for me at least. Firstly, I am introverted by nature and to say that being emotionally expressive was uncomfortable for me would have been a gross under-statement. Secondly, it felt fake and inauthentic. How could I possibly express happiness and confidence when I wasn't feeling so?

To overcome my first reservation, I remembered the following quote from Einstein — "Insanity is doing the same things over and over again and expecting a different result". If I was to get out of the rut I was in, I had to start forming new habits and doing things differently, even if it meant getting out of my comfort zone. My addiction to comfort and security had contributed to my being in the situation I was in — it certainly wasn't going to lead me out of it! I was sick of being an unfulfilled achiever and wanted instead to live and realise my highest potential.

To overcome my second reservation, I asked myself, "When I'm not feeling happy or confident, is it possible that it is due to the habits I have developed rather than the 'authentic' me? What is the authentic me anyway?" I remembered that my authentic original self, the child I was before I developed habits through social conditioning, was happy and confident, adaptable, curious and full of life! Could it be that I had conditioned myself to be insecure and anxious? That who I was and the emotions I was experiencing wasn't the "authentic" me after all, but the mask I had been wearing and the rituals I had formed, to protect myself? If I was to overcome this conditioning, it would take time and persistent practise. That's how any new habit is formed. When doing something new initially, it feels uncomfortable. But that doesn't make it wrong.

Take folding your arms as an example. Go ahead and fold your arms right now. Notice which hand is above the other. Now unfold your arms. Then fold your arms again. Did you fold your arms the same way? If so, why did you do so? Because it was comfortable, right? Unfold your arms. Now fold your arms again, but this time, consciously do so with the other arm above the other. How does that feel? Not quite as comfortable right? Does that mean it's the wrong way to fold your arms? Of course it isn't. But it's just not comfortable. If I were to get you to fold your arms again, quickly, without hesitation, how would you fold your arms? The new way or the old way? Chances are, you'd go back to old way right? Why? The power of a habit. Our habits are designed to make us comfortable. But remember this, comfort or safety does not equal fulfilment. Fulfilment comes from meaningful growth towards our highest potential, to enable us to find and utilise our talents to make the biggest difference to ourselves and those around us. But imagine if I were to get you to fold your arms, repeatedly for say, 21 times in the new way. After 21 times, if I were to snap my fingers and say, "fold your arms", how might you do it? The new way right?

So I surmised that if I were to start experiencing life to the fullest, I needed to use this science to start making the change. And best of all, this change was totally within my control. I took to heart the advice Amy Cuddy gives others through her wonderful TED talk — "fake it till you make it![22]"

As I'd previously shared, I started moving differently, walking into the office every day in a much more energetic, confident and positive manner. I decided to be cheerful and smile more. I looked at others confidently and with love in my heart and this invariably attracted a similar response, which made me feel even more positive.

At the end of every work day, just before I reached my front door, I'd pause for a moment to reflect on what would make the evening the most extraordinary experience and then open the door and stride in with positive energy, love and an enthusiastic "Hey, how's everybody? How was your day?" My days and evenings started to be so positive.

My wife and I had been through the workshops together and together we resolved to consciously create and condition positive emotional states into our family. Whenever we felt the need for a lift in the spirits of our family, we'd crank up some music and start moving enthusiastically to the beat. Dance and movement can have a therapeutic affect on stress and just creates that much more fun in our lives. I am truly happy that all three of my children dance and exercise regularly. It's such a positive and constructive habit to have and I know this helps them cope with stress and change in a positive way.

I started a regular exercise program, initially just three 30-minute walks a day. I made modifications to my diet, becoming even more conscious of hydrating myself well, eating more raw vegetables and fruits, and investing in quality nutritional supplements. While in some cases, the results were instantaneous, others took some patience and persistence. After about a month of doing this, I started to feel considerably more positive and what's more, others started to notice. This spiral of positivity in turn affected not just me but others around me in a most positive way.

Having turned what was initially uncomfortable then, to not just comfortable but indeed incredibly pleasurable today, such habits have been conditioned deep into my subconscious. My brain has indeed been rewired. Whenever I feel stress coming on, I subconsciously smile, take a deep breath, walk, or sleep it off before I make a decision.

At the beginning of last year, my beautiful daughter Courtney started Year 10 and in a new school. A week into the school year, she came home one day and asked me if I could review some homework she'd completed and give her my opinion. She had been asked to write a one-page autobiography for her English subject and was to present this to class the next day. She started her piece by writing about her family and how it was by far the biggest influence in her life. She introduced me as, "Dad, whose name is Dominic, also known as the happiest person you'll ever meet". Reading this brought tears to my eyes. I realised that my life had come full circle. I had started to embrace these practices, in truth, for my personal benefit, so I could feel better and more fulfilled about my life. And with the deepest intent to ultimately enable me to touch more lives more positively. To know how my daughter truly felt about me was so validating.

Today, I couldn't be more authentic about feeling extraordinarily blessed and empowered. I move, think and speak mostly in an empowered, positive way because that's how I genuinely feel and it's become who I am. I've become this way due to the wonderful new habits I've formed to alter every aspect of my life, out of a determination to strive to be the very best self I can be. You can too, and you deserve no less! Even if you felt this was too uncomfortable, if all you take from this chapter is the deep profound realisation that how you think, feel and act is not a factor of your environment but that you alone have the power to choose this, and to choose to be a master of your destiny rather than a victim of your circumstances, this decision alone will help you be more empowered and resilient in the face of disruption and chance. I still get many moments of reactive self-doubt, where the first instinct is to blame and brood and get anxious. But today, the big difference is that I know this is a choice I am making. And I choose deliberately not to stay in that place for too long by using the techniques in this chapter to change my state to something more empowering.

In the words of the amazing Gandhi — *"Be the change you wish to see in this world."*

Action Plan

Make a commitment today to incorporate some or all of the following into regular rituals:

- Start each day with a two-minute power pose.

- Establish eye contact and smile at people you meet.

- Make it a goal to bring a smile to at least three people every day.

- Take a break every 60-90 minutes to take a brisk walk, rehydrate, and do 10 deep abdominal breaths.

- If you don't already have one, decide to formulate a regular physical exercise routine. Preferably create one that combines elements of aerobic (e.g. walking, running, cycling, swimming, rowing or using the elliptical machines), strength (e.g. using weights or simply your body weight) and stretching (yoga, Pilates, qi-gong, etc.). Be sure to get proper coaching on the right form whenever you exercise and also on how you should breathe.

- To create and project energy and confidence (also called "presence"), stride purposefully and strongly into your workplace and into every meeting.

- If you're not already into meditation, download and take the Take10 Headspace challenge.

- Review your diet and make a decision to add natural food that's rich with vitamins, minerals, omega oils and water content to your diet e.g. vegetables, fruits and nuts, while cutting down on processed food that has chemical preservatives and additives including processed sugar.

- Decide to shut down the technology at least an hour before you go to bed. Get to bed earlier and for at least a week, work out how much sleep you ideally need. You can do this by sleeping without setting an alarm clock. When you wake up, if you feel rested and energised, that's probably the optimal amount of sleep you need. Then make sure you get that amount of sleep every day.

Share this with one of your best mates, someone who will hold you accountable to making this a conscious habit for at least 21 days until it becomes second nature and part of who you are and how you show up every day!

CHAPTER 6

How Resilient People Talk

The words you use and how you express yourself affects your emotional state

Be aware and choose language patterns that empower you

Make the chanting of empowering affirmations part of your daily ritual

Stop negative self-talk or making excuses

Turn your commute into time for your personal development

"Words are pale shadows of forgotten names. As names have power, words have power. Words can light fires in the minds of men. Words can wring tears from the hardest hearts."

— Patrick Rothfuss, The Name of the Wind

"But if thought corrupts language, language can also corrupt thought."

— George Orwell, 1984

Using positive affirmations

[1]Our self-talk, the choice of words we use and how we express ourselves is another habit that affects the way we feel. In fact, it also affects the emotional state of others around us.

When someone asks you how your day is, how do you typically respond? Try using the word "average" and expressing it that way. Do it right now. How does that feel? How about an upbeat 'GREAT!" How does that feel?

Isn't it great to know that we can pretty much create any emotion we want just by using words that convey that emotion and expressing it like we mean it?

If I'm not feeling confident and I'd like to, I can simply say "I **AM** CONFIDENT!" like I mean it and instantly experience confidence. And so it is with love, fun, joy, and gratitude ... any emotional state you choose to create.

For each of the empowering emotional states you've chosen to be and create each and every day, I encourage you to develop the habit of daily affirmations. Repeating a particular uplifting, inspiring phrase over and over again like you mean it has been shown to be a powerful way to ensure it's ingrained ("conditioned") into your neurology.

Our brain is much like a CD and our habitual beliefs and meanings we give to events that happen around us are the mental tapes that are unconsciously played again and again, affecting our emotions, actions and outcomes. Affirmations are a powerful way to reprogram empowering thoughts and beliefs into your brain, displacing disempowering thought patterns that were previously ingrained. Have you ever heard a favourite tune over and over again and when you turned the music off, the tune stayed in your head over the course of the next few hours or day? That's the effect that affirmations can have on you.

When I learned this, I was astounded by how easily I could turn any disempowering emotional state I was in, into a positive state. I was determined to put this into practise, using affirmations both for short-term state change as well as longer term reconditioning of my neurology until getting into this state became as natural and easy as drawing breath!

A new ritual I developed 15 years ago was to perform the following affirmations every morning and whenever I felt I needed a boost:

"I am courage! I am faith! I am love! I am fun!"

I'd repeat the above 10 times, reciting each word with feeling, intensity and congruent movement of my body. Until I felt and believed every word and phrase. For instance, I would clench my fists and pump my fists at the word "courage", close my eyes and soften my tone when I used the words "faith" and "love" and put a huge smile on my face, look upwards and raise my hands with my palms upwards when I said "fun".

I'd then do the following for another 10 repeats:

"All I need is within me now! Every day in every way, I'm getting better and better. When the going gets tough, the tough get going and they don't get tougher than ME!"

This would put me in such a positive energy state that I'd feel ready to conquer the world!

I still remember learning about this during a weekend retreat. I was so motivated by this that I decided there and then to start being more conscious of using positive vocabulary and expressing myself in congruence with those words. I saw these simply as tools to make myself feel more empowered and knew that if I felt that way, it would have a positive effect on my actions and thus create better outcomes not just for me but for others around me.

So the very next day I was in the office when I received a phone call. I picked it up with a cheery, "Hi! This is Dom! Who do I have the pleasure of connecting with?" When I was asked, "How are you?" instead of "Not bad, thanks", I said "Just a shade of PHENOMENAL!" with a huge grin on my face. This elicited a hearty laugh from the other end and drew a few chuckles from my colleagues sitting close to my cubicle. I felt what others must have been thinking — "Hmm. He's in a cheery mood" and it dawned on me I could make a positive impact on not only my emotional state but on those of the folks around me just by expressing positivity.

Now, if you do decide to put this into practise, a word of warning: You might get a few weird stares and experience the occasional put-downs. When I first did this, I remember a guy at the far end of the office calling out, "You're full of shit, mate!"

That didn't discourage me though. I wasn't doing it to impress anyone, just to transform the way I felt about life and in the process make a positive impact to those around me. Know that many of the people around us aren't living up to their highest potential. They're driven by security and comfort and don't necessarily want others around them to be different. They'll often be the first to try and shut you down.

I've learned that you can't please everyone all of the time. In fact, in your quest to being the finest leader you can be, firstly of your life and then others around you, you must be able to make doing "what's right" more important than doing "what's popular". After all, the very best of the best leaders of all time – be it Gandhi or Mandela – have their haters, so why not us?

[2]Dr John Demartini, another wise philosopher and trainer I admire and have learned a lot from said, "You would have mastered your life when the voices from the inside are louder than the voices from the outside". Meaning, if you've tried out these techniques and strategies and they work, they make you feel better, and if a huge reason you want to feel better is so you can do better for others around you, then don't be discouraged by others just because how you are being is not the norm. Don't be afraid to stand out for doing the right thing!

So, instead of feeling discouraged, I said, "Thanks for that feedback mate. Sorry to be a distraction. I'll tone down my volume a notch." I kept doing it with the same amount of passion and enthusiasm, and just lowered my volume out of consideration for others. I've been doing this for 15 years now and it's just wonderful regularly getting comments and drawing chuckles from those I greet, in addition to keeping me in the most empowered state I choose to be in. This decision would be another in many decisions that would kick-start my transformation and journey towards the bright future I chose to have.

Since that day, I've been conscious of the habitual choice of words and body language I use to express myself. I grew up in a family where men, in particular, were not expected to be very expressive with their emotions. However, I've since learned effective communication is largely not a result of the choice of words we use but how we express ourselves. Note that by being expressive, I'm not suggesting you be emotional. The latter is a phrase generally associated with emotions such as anger and frustration and is generally unhelpful both for you and others around you. By being expressive, I mean choosing language that is more empowering and expressing yourself through the use of congruent tone and body language.

Knowing that the most important person I get to influence every day is me, why not use this as a tool to get myself in the best possible state? Best of all, it's free of charge!

Whenever you're feeling disempowered, know that it could be your choice of vocabulary and expression that could be putting you in that state. Develop a greater sensitivity towards this and start expressing yourself in a way that makes you feel empowered.

Imagine someone saying to you over and over again each and every day, "I like your CONFIDENCE." "You are LOVE." "You are KINDNESS." "You are PASSION." Do you think some of that would stick? You bet!

I also find that using empowering language not only helps me feel bet-ter, it's such a powerful way to influence the way others feel. Whenever I used to greet my friends, I would do the standard, "Hello, how are you?" These days, regardless of whether it's on the phone, face-to-face or through email, my standard greeting is "How's the SENSATIONAL/AMAZING/OUTSTANDING/EXTRAORDINARY Angela doing?"

Some who don't know me well may think I'm just a super positive but insincere bloke. But those who do know me well will understand that over the past 15 years, I've seen and experienced first-hand how amazing we humans truly are and what we're capable of.

Consider the man who was born without limbs and even considered taking his life, and now inspires millions all over the world with what's possible, or the grandmother who once lifted a one-tonne truck to save a child. The words that I use to describe how truly extraordinary I feel about the people around me do not do them justice. So when I use those adjectives to describe others, I actually am understating, not overstating how I truly feel about them!

I was once the captain of my university badminton team. We had a marvellous team, one that had won the title three years in a row, and we were aiming for our fourth. I was particularly keen to achieve this record not just because it would have meant a clean slate for every year I represented the university, but for sentimental reasons. That year, I had my youngest brother Ben on my team as well and winning one for Team Siow would have been a memory to cherish indeed.

We made it to the finals where we would be facing our great rivals for the championship – the team from Monash University. Competing over seven matches (four singles and three doubles), both teams knew that match #4 was particularly crucial. We expected a very close encounter given we both had singles players who were of a very similar standard. The night before the big game, my fourth singles team mate, Michael, came up to me and suggested he might do better focussing just on the doubles in the finals as he was nursing a minor injury. I sensed that the injury and the pressure of this particular tie was really starting to get to him. I was in a quandary — while I felt Michael could acquit himself quite well over both ties, to field him when he wasn't entirely confident could mean risking him losing not just that match but his doubles tie as well.

I decided to raise the issue with the team during our final team meeting for their open debate. Our fifth singles, a Thai national by the name of Somkiat, was a cheerful, reliable sort. A keen and competent tennis player, he had taken up badminton later in life and while he could hold a good game, didn't have the experience or polished skills of an established player like Michael, who had competed from a young age. Eight times out of 10 in practise, Michael would have won playing against Somkiat.

So you can only imagine the mood in the room when I dropped the bombshell that Michael was not quite up to taking on the fourth singles slot that day. I looked at Somkiat and said, "Somkiat, how do *you* feel about taking on this challenge?" Knowing the conservative nature of most from an Asian cultural heritage, I expected him to either say he wasn't ready for the challenge or at best "I'll try my best". Instead, his face broke out in a wide grin, his eyes simply lit up and he said, "Why not?" Those two words lifted the entire mood in the room. Everyone started to slap him on the back and told him how much we believed he could do this.

When it was time to contest the fourth singles, the Monash player hit the court early. Going through his warm-up rituals in public, he seemed to be communicating to the world, "I've got this under control". When

Somkiat walked on, I watched his opponent's body language closely. My first reading was that he was confused. I think he would have mentally prepared himself to face Michael, who he'd also met and beaten in an earlier round. And then I sensed the pressure building in him. His previous confidence was replaced with tension as he felt the expectations of his team weigh down on him, with him now being the obvious favourite to win the tie.

Somkiat played like a champion. A crowd pleaser, he rose to the challenge, returning every shot and owning the court like he belonged, which he truly did. He beat an overly-cautious opponent in three hard games. That match taught me that being positive and expressing positivity can have a far-reaching impact on both yourself and those around you.

Another word I've learned to eradicate from my vocabulary whenever I'm given a challenge or asked to do anything is "try". While my stock standard response in the past would have been, "I'll try", today, my response if I accept the challenge is either, "Consider it done!" or "You can count on my 100% best effort!" Imagine if this were subconscious habit. Could this potentially affect the decision made by a superior or customer, which could then potentially impact the rest of your life? Imagine you have two staff members, one who habitually says, "I'll try", and another who says, "Consider it done," and you only have one spot in your team. Who might you pick?

Decide today to develop the habit of saying, "Why not?" to any oppor-tunity that may present itself to you! Master the negativity bias through conscious choice of the words you use and how you express yourself, and learn to use this tool of language powerfully to create the most empowering emotional state for yourself.

Action

Come up with a set of 10 to 12 favourite affirmations that express posi-tivity and put you in the most empowering state. Decide today to repeat those phrases again and again (10 repetitions, three times a day) with emotional intensity. Say it until you BECOME it.

Here are some of my favourites:

- "Every day in every way, I am getting better and better."
- "Life works with me and for me."
- "I am love."
- "I am courage."
- "I am faith."
- "I am fun."
- "I achieve anything I set my mind to."
- "When the going gets tough, the tough get going."
- "I'm the captain of my ship, the master of my soul."

In summary, the words you habitually use and how you express your-self affects your emotions. Learn to embrace empowering, positive language in every situation in life. Instead of "I'll try", learn to say, "Consider it done!" with confidence. Instead of "That's a problem", say, "I'm up for the challenge!" And proactively use affirmations every day and in every situation where you feel you can benefit from a great pick-me-up!

Stories and how we nourish our minds

"Whether you think you can or you cannot, you are absolutely right"

– Henry Ford

[3]Resilient people are conscious of their self-talk and selective about how they nourish one of their most important muscles – their thoughts. Along with the choice of words you use and how you express yourself, you should also be aware of the stories you tell yourself again and again.

Sometimes you'll hear a person say, "but I don't think I can" or "change is difficult" or "I'm not great with change" or "you don't understand … when I was young, such and such was my situation". Listen to them give you a litany of reasons to back these up. The "reasoning" they give is what I call the disempowering stories we feed our minds that in turn affect the way we feel and our actions during times of change.

To change the way we respond to change, we need to break negative patterns of disempowering stories that stop us from being more resilient. Let me share with you an example of how stories can powerfully influence our decisions and behaviours.

Chip and Dan Heath, authors of *Made to Stick*[1] — a wonderful book about change, share a story that goes like this:

"A guy who's on a business trip in Las Vegas gets to a bar after a hard day's work. He's lonely and feeling pretty exhausted. A beautiful blonde walks up to him flashing a great smile and invites him to have a drink with her. He does. And that's the last he remembers of that evening.

When he regains consciousness, he finds himself disrobed and immersed in a bathtub full of ice. Alarmed, he sees a sign by the side of the bathtub that reads 'DON'T MOVE! RING 911'. He calls the number, describes his predicament to the person on the hotline and is surprised that she doesn't seem overly surprised. She asks him to reach out his right hand towards the lower part of his back and to see if he could find a tube protruding from the region where his kidney is. To his surprise, he finds there is. He's instructed not to move and is assured that an ambulance was on its way. He's informed that he's been a victim of a kidney heist — that a syndicate had been operating in the city, preying on unsuspecting visitors, harvesting their kidneys and then selling them on the black market for organs."

Have you heard this story or something close to it before? Let me ask you this – if you were male and visiting Las Vegas in the near future, went to a bar and a lady walked up to you with a similar proposal, what might you do?

Stories are incredibly impactful in driving human behaviour. What stories do you have a habit of telling yourself over and over again? Have you heard of those who lament that they could achieve everything they wanted in life if only their children were older, if not for the previous recession, if only their parents had left them an inheritance and so on. Such stories create deeply set beliefs that become huge invisible barriers to your potential success.

I'm sure you've also heard of people with the very same life experiences but who took so much positive energy and lessons from those incidents that they made their lives an absolute masterpiece. These people choose to dwell on all the stories in their lives that empower them – stories about changes that occurred and how they not only survived these changes but how they got even better, wiser, and stronger because of them.

If you've been wallowing in such disempowering stories in the past, start focussing instead on all the times you overcame great adversity. Focus on when you achieved something you or others didn't think possible. Talk up your wins and all the attributes you have that put you in such a great position to achieve the goal you've set yourself.

Make it a regular habit to reflect on the following questions:

"What's GREAT about my life?"

"What's GREAT about me?

Action Plan

Start a Gratitude Log and write down a list of the positive attributes, skills, experiences, successes resources and expertise you have:

- Kick-ass attributes like determination (you wouldn't be reading this far if you didn't have that!), faith and discipline (which you exercise every day doing what's important to you even if you didn't feel like it).

- Skills (technical or interpersonal).

- Experiences (including previous examples of when you achieved something you didn't think you were capable of).

- Resources (people, contacts, relationships, assets, finances, knowledge, tools, books).

Choosing what you feed your mind

Your mindset is the most powerful factor that determines how you cope in times of uncertainty. It's also the most powerful tool you can tap into, to thrive with the opportunities presented by any change.

Your mind is just like any other muscle you have — it takes regular conditioning and nourishment for it to serve you at its highest capacity. Just like we're careful about what we eat, it's important to also be very careful about what we feed our minds.

The media today is constantly bombarding us with negative stories that incite fear, disillusionment, cynicism, and even depression. Negative stories sell lots of papers but don't do much to condition our mind for success and fulfilment.

Be judicious about what you feed your mind. Cultivate the habit of reading stories, watching documentaries, videos, podcasts, audiobooks or movies that empower you with positive lessons, lift your spirit and help you achieve your goals.

Turn this into a regular habit. Just as it's difficult to maintain a high level of fitness only by going to the gym every now and then, create rituals to feed your mind and keep it in tip-top shape. Here are some practical suggestions on how you can continually condition your mind with stories that empower and strengthen you:

- Turn commute time (whether this be in the car, train, bus or plane) into your "commute university". Instead of listening to the radio, use your valuable time to listen to music with uplifting, inspiring lyrics and great audiobooks or podcasts from role models of resilience, positivity, and optimism. If you're interested in checking out some of my favourite authors, podcasts and articles, visit this website - www.eqstrategist.com/resources.html.

- Embrace the habit of reading. Leaders are readers. Amazon is full of e-books and paper books that you can purchase relatively inexpensively. If you search the Internet, chances are you'll also access great blogs or download lots of materials for free from any of the authors above. In addition, I subscribe to and love the work of Brian Johnson[5], who produces book summaries and short video logs. Again, you can check out my personal favourites which I update regularly using the following link - www.eqstrategist.com/resources.html.

Action Plan

Decide today to be more conscious of how you nourish your mind. Make reading or listening to great books, stories, blogs and podcasts about resilient, positivity, and inspiring people a daily ritual. There's a wealth of e-books, videos and audiobooks that you can listen to during your commute to work or while exercising. Take one action today to start building this lifelong, positive habit of continuous and positive improvement.

CHAPTER 7

How Resilient People Think

Resilient people are both realistic and optimistic

The difference between optimism and denial optimism

Don't ask the "Blame Why"

Reflecting on "What's GREAT about this?"

Cultivating an attitude of Gratitude

Getting beyond "Freeze"

"The pessimist complains about the wind; the optimist expects it to change; the realist adjusts the sails."

– William Arthur Ward

Getting beyond "Freeze"

As a frequent traveller, I use taxis a lot. Given my mission in life is to make the world a better place by helping people feel better about themselves so they can serve their highest potential and the greater good, I usually hop into the front seat when I get into a cab. The poor cabbie doesn't realise this but he or she is about to get a free 30-minute coaching session.

After some small talk to break the ice, I'd typically ask, "How's life?" Nine times of 10, this would open up a huge lament about the poor state of the economy, how the government was making life harder for them by raising taxes, allowing Uber, approving for more taxis to hit the streets, higher petrol prices etc. They'd tell me about how they're having to work so much harder than before. Many cabbies in countries like Malaysia, the UAE and Singapore drive 16 hours a day, seven days a week to meet quotas, pay off expensive taxi rentals, and bring home a meagre wage — struggling to make ends meet as the cost of living soars.

When I say to them, "How do you find time to exercise?" a typical response is, "What exercise? No time to exercise man! I get home, my head hits the pillow and its lights out! No time." And then I say, "Driving and sitting for long hours isn't great for your health. What if a doctor says to you one day 'You have high blood pressure. You need to slow down?'" A sense of helplessness often emerges "What do I do? I have no choice." One cabbie, a father of four said, "Sir, I don't want to think about it. I cannot imagine going a day without work as I won't be able to afford to pay the bills and feed my children." With a note of resignation, they'll typically add, "But you know, it's actually not that bad. At least I have a job. I'm actually quite satisfied with my lot in life."

Who do you think is more adaptable and resilient in the face of change or adversity – the pessimist, optimist or realist?

When I ask this question in many of my workshops, most say the optimist. My journey has taught me that to be resilient and adaptable, you must be both a realist and an optimist. The dictionary informs me that a realist is a person who looks at the facts, sees things as they are and deals with it in a practical manner. It's no good being optimistic if that means adopting a "she'll be right" attitude and thinking the problem will go away. This is typical of many cabbies as painted in the scenario above, and it's what I call *optimistic denial*. If you're faced with a challenge, chances are it isn't going to go away. Just hoping for the best without making any attempt to exercise your resourcefulness and creativity to make things better will ultimately only lead to even greater pain in my opinion.

Figure 11 - Optimistic Denial (Image Credit: Andrew Grossman ©123RF.com)

Change is hard for many and it's worth reminding ourselves of the frog in the pot story.

When you put a live frog into a pot of boiling water, how do you think it'll react? It'll jump out right? But what if you put this frog into pot of cool water and gently brought it up to boil? What do you think it'll do? It will start to feel uncomfortable but after awhile it'll just keep swimming thinking, "Hey, it's getting warm in here. But there's nothing I can do about it. I'm tough. It's ok". And truly just like the frog, we are, from a survival standpoint, more robust than we give ourselves credit for. But what do you think eventually happens to the frog? Yes, it cooks! Optimistic denial is certainly not a great strategy for being resilient and thriving with change.

As a migrant to Australia whose parents still live overseas in Malaysia, one of the greatest fears I used to have was receiving that late night phone call. I received such a call about 15 years ago and it was my youngest brother Ben. He told me that dad had gotten really ill. Dad was 65 at the time, and had been vomiting and suffering from severe abdominal pain for several days. He couldn't hold down anything he'd consumed. After many inconclusive tests, dad was finally wheeled in for major surgery. Apparently, he had just signed a form acknowledging that there was a chance he might not get out of the surgery alive. I was shocked. In all my years of knowing dad, I'd seldom ever seen the man unwell. I couldn't remember him ever taking a sickie in his life and I definitely didn't remember him ever being hospitalised. And now, the very first time he was going in, we were faced with the possibility it could be his last.

I booked the next flight home. Hoping for the best, I had decided with my brothers Chris and Ben that we'd take turns spending time at home to help with dad's recuperation.

When I got to the hospital in my hometown of Seremban, Malaysia, I learned that the surgeon had made a 12-inch incision to my dad's abdomen and opened him up, fully expecting to find something sinister. Not able to find anything amiss, they had simply stitched him up and ordered more tests. Seeing my dad in so much pain was difficult to say the least.

Dad had many dear friends and family visit him in hospital during that period. One of his contemporaries and good friend, John, was a devout Christian, a kind, lovely man who himself had recovered from heart surgery many years prior. During one of his visits, he overheard me suggesting to my dad that instead of just sitting around waiting for more tests at an undetermined time, we should seek a second opinion and explore our options. I've learned that the results we get in life are not a factor of the resources we have, but our resourcefulness. I was determined to fully tap into all the knowledge, contacts, and resources that I had to give my dad the best chance for a quick and full recovery.

Given the generation gap between John and I, I suspect I would have come across to him as someone who was overly exuberant and perhaps he felt my enthusiasm was putting more stress on my dad. He said, in almost an irritated manner, "Don't worry. Have faith. God knows best. Let's just pray."

Now, I'm all for praying. I truly believe the positive thoughts we put out are not just an expression of our faith but also a form of positive energy, and we attract what we think about the most. If praying means exercising faith, and putting out every intention and thought of how we'll be when we've fully recovered, I'm all for it. But that should not preclude every other course of meaningful action we could take. That shouldn't make us lazy or unresourceful. Using the words of St Augustine, "Pray as though everything depended on God. Work as though everything depended on you"[1].

So, it's important to distinguish between optimism and denial optimism. The optimism that really helps isn't the kind that stops at "she'll be right" but the kind that has the deep knowing that something good can arise from every situation and focuses on taking constructive, positive action towards our preferred outcome. This starts by realising first and foremost that as in the story of the frog in the pot, the flame (which represents "change") isn't going to go off. The realist researches the facts to understand the change better and uses this reality to create a healthy dose of intrinsically-motivated urgency to propel one forward towards their desired future.

In my dad's situation, the facts were:

1. Doctors seemed uncertain about what they ought to do. If they were, they were certainly poor in communicating their plans to us. Repeated attempts to contact them were met with, "they're busy right now."

2. They were ordering more tests, and the earliest the tests could be done would be in a week.

3. They had already done a battery of tests, which had been inconclusive.

4. The technology in this particular hospital wasn't the best.

5. My dad was experiencing great discomfort.

6. In the best-case scenario, dad's condition would not get worse and the tests would reveal the root cause of the issue and then further interventions would be scheduled. This would take at least a couple of weeks of severe pain for my dad.

7. In the worst-case scenario, my dad's condition would worsen. He would be too weak, physically and mentally by the time they decided to intervene.

8. We could not hasten events at the hospital – they were simply overloaded and had other situations they deemed to require more critical attention.

These facts were sufficient to convince me that there was certainly much more we could do to make the progress we wanted towards an ideal outcome. After seeking the second opinion of several doctors we trusted, we were able to get an accurate diagnosis of the root cause of dad's problem – gall bladder stones that had resulted in a badly inflamed pancreas and a painful condition called pancreatitis. Through a procedure to remove his gall bladder, dad was finally relieved of his debilitating pain and was able to stage a full recovery, bringing much relief not just to dad but to those around him.

I also applied this philosophy to the change affecting me at my workplace. I decided that instead of judging the restructure as a "power move" by my superiors and throwing up my hands in despair thinking there was nothing I could do about it, I would give them the benefit of the doubt and research the underlying facts that brought about the restructure. My research helped me understand the following facts:

1. Our business model, which depended on selling more software products to clients and then services to implement and use it effectively, was unsustainable in the face of declining software licensing prices and increased competition.

2. The restructure process had already commenced. There was no turning back. Nothing I could do would change that.

3. Complaining and adopting passive-aggressive behaviour was having an adverse impact on my reality at the time, along with that of my team. This would affect my future prospects in the organisation and the confidence my leadership team had in me.

Being realistic and confronting the brutal facts helped me get out of denial and start my journey of recovery and moving forward. It got me focussed on "what can I do about this?" rather than dwelling on the "Blame Why". It reinforced to me the value of having the mindset that I cannot change the change, and that no one is going to be more interested or able to make things better for me, than me.

Action Plan

Think about a workplace challenge or change you are going through right now. Reflect on the following:

- Do you have control over those factors driving the need for change?

- What level of influence do you have over the change that has already occurred?

- Would your attempts to influence create positive or negative energy?

- Are there better ways to create positivity and channel positive energy at this time?

Stop Asking the "Blame Why"!!

"Life inflicts the same setbacks and tragedies on the optimist as on the pessimist, but the optimist weathers it better."
— *Dr Martin Seligman*

[2]Optimists are happier, more resilient and generally more successful than pessimists. Whether one is an optimist or pessimist can actually be measured by what Dr Martin Seligman calls our explanatory style. This is how we "explain" or give meaning to events that occur in our lives. Dr Seligman, Director of the University of Pennsylvania's Positive Psychology Centre and also author of the New York Times best-seller "Learned Optimism[3]" devised and validated the Seligman Attributional Style Questionnaire or SASQ, an instrument that assesses one's

explanatory style. [4]In 1990, Dr Seligman and his colleagues (Seligman, Nolen-Hoeksema, Thornton, & Thornton, 1990) conducted a study of nationally ranked swimmers from the University of California. They found that those athletes who scored as pessimistic felt defeated by false feedback from their coaches, who told them they had posted slower times than they actually did. Their performance deteriorated on a second swim. Performance decrements were not shown by swimmers who scored as optimists.

[5]In research done with insurance salespeople at Metropolitan Life, they found that even when sales aptitude was taken into account, the most optimistic salespeople sold 37% more insurance in their initial two years in the business when compared with their more pessimistic counterparts.

Things that happen around us have no meaning apart from the meaning we give them — what Dr Seligman terms our explanatory style. If an earthquake happens, we can say, "Geez, that sucks. Life is so unpredictable. What's the point in planning?" Or we could say, "Geez, I'm so blessed not to be living in that area." So how do we give things meaning? One of the tools we subconsciously use to do this is the *question or series of questions* we use in our self-talk. Do you realise that we ask questions in our head all the time? Yes. And you thought you were the only one who did that right? It's our conscious mind's way of making sense of things that happen around us. And the questions we ask tend also to be habitual.

Here's what I've learned. The question that often results in answers that put us in a disempowered state is usually the "Blame Why" question.

The flavour of *why* asked in an accusatory tone and that often results in blame. It's the *why* that assumes whatever happened is not good e.g. "Why me? Why did that happen? Why did you do that?"

My conclusion and advice to you is this: Don't ask the "Blame Why?"

Now I realise some of you may be thinking, surely "why" is a good question to ask. After all, we should be learning from every situation, right? Yes, you're absolutely right. But do keep in mind that communication is not just about what you say but how you say it. *Why* asked in a negative "blame" tone is disempowering. *Why* expressed from a source of genuine curiosity, the "Curious Why" is empowering. The "Blame Why" happens to be the version that pessimists and whiners habitually use a lot.

We certainly weren't born with this trait. It's something we've most likely learned. A child learning to crawl does not bump its head on the table and ask, "why?" The child will just rub its head, cry a little perhaps, take the positive lesson and move on! I personally think that most of us have subconsciously developed this habit from our upbringing and environment. Be conscious that most people live in "blame-ville." Everything that happens in their lives is often other people's fault. Ever been in an environment like that? I know growing up I was often in the receiving end of accusations such as, "Why didn't you study? Why didn't you turn the lights off? Why did you lie? Why…" I detested it, and yet I came to realise that I was also doing that a lot to others too.

When I was feeling disempowered during those two dark years, guess which question I was constantly asking? Yes, you're right. It was

"WHY is this happening to me?" Our brains are our slaves, there to do as we command them. It's not the brain, but the operating system running it that drives behaviour. If the operating system churns out the "Blame Why" in response to the inputs from the environment, it will reliably visit our database of experiences and come up with answers. The problem is – how do you think the answers make you feel? Empowered or disempowered? Yes, you're right! Disempowered!

I was getting answers like, "My AP Director doesn't care about people. They pay lip service to 'people are our most important asset'. The bottom line is **all** that matters in business. You're just another number, a statistic in this business. There's no loyalty in business." How do you think such answers made me feel? When you feel disempowered, what actions do you take? For me, it was putting myself in a state of helplessness and blame. I was blaming my manager and the company for the state I was in and for the state my team was in, and that made me feel like I was a victim. This wouldn't have been lost on my leadership team who were looking for resilient, positive types to drive the team forward in the new structure.

So whenever you're feeling distressed or disempowered in any situation, press the pause button and reflect on that inner voice. What question is it asking? What are you dwelling on? Another problem with the *why* question is that it sets your focus on the past and on the problem. And when that's what you focus on, you're not focussed on the solution, the blessing, or opportunities presented in that situation.

So, in short, stop the "Blame Why!"

Now, I know you may be thinking. Shouldn't we be investigating the causes of a particular event? And isn't "why" a natural and in fact, very constructive question to ask when we're in that situation?

ABSOLUTELY.

[6]Research on humanistic psychology reveals that everything we do, we do because we're driven to meet our physiological (food, water, sleep and sex) and psychological needs.[7] Abraham Maslow, who studied, who for the last 30 years has dedicated his life to studying and empowering others on human motivation and behaviour, says that everything we do, we do to meet six psychological needs. The first is the need for certainty or security.

No matter where we come from (and I've asked this question of participants over 11 different countries now), no one likes nasty surprises. Our brain's most basic function is survival, and over time, we've associated survival with "comfort". Our rituals or routines make us feel comfortable which is why we generally don't like anything we envisage messes with our routine. In situations where we either believe or feel our comfort may be threatened, we have developed habitual coping strategies that help us seize control. The "Blame Why" that many ask during times of uncertainty is simply a habitual strategy they have developed for meeting this need for certainty in times of change.

The need for security or certainty is one of four needs Robbins calls the needs of our personality or ego. The others are the need for variety (surprises of the nice kind – think adventure, spontaneity, hobbies, anything that breaks routine), significance (or self-esteem needs, to feel we're important and that we matter) and love (to feel connected and a sense of belonging). If we put our need for security over all other needs and if we rely on our work routine, or position, as a vehicle to meet this need, then we may well "survive". But we're not likely to be happy or fulfilled. The focus on survival creates stress in our lives and we don't respond best when we're stressed.

Our two highest order needs, also known as our spiritual needs, are to grow (to continually improve mentally, emotionally and spiritually) and to contribute (to serve a higher purpose or to make the lives of others better in some way, to leave a legacy). [8]Abraham Maslow, who studied people who were happy and fulfilled over a number of years found that beyond basic survival needs, humans have an innate need to self-actualise, to realise or fulfil our highest potential. As humans, we derive a great sense of personal satisfaction, inner peace and joy through the process of, and the pursuit of our worthy ideals. It's not what we get that gives us the deep sense of lasting happiness we seek, but the journey towards it, who we become, who we get to meet, who we get to impact in a positive way, and our life experiences along the journey that gives us fulfilment.

So all of us have the same needs, and yet the value we place on one or the other varies in each phase of our life. Someone who values certainty over growth and who gets their certainty from their job routine, will certainly respond very differently to change when compared with someone who values growth. One will try to seek control over a situation that is often beyond their control and end up stressed and unhappy. They'll typically ask the "Blame Why", feel disempowered and project negative energy. The person who values growth over certainty sees each event as an opportunity to learn, to become even better, to *be* more in a way that empowers the person with the skills and confidence to achieve even more. This person will typically ask, "What's the positive lesson in this?" or "What's great about this?"

[9]In essence, resilient people are learning or growth-oriented as opposed to comfort or security-oriented. They are always focussed on the positive lesson presented in every situation. They're pragmatic in knowing they can't control the environment, and yet they have total control over what they can learn from any situation. They're inquisitive and always asking the "Curious Why". The "Curious Why" puts them into an empowered state. Growth-oriented people become curious rather than angry, resentful, or frustrated. They're open to options and doors that could help them thrive and that invariably arise in every change, while whiners are closed off, myopic and often times shut down.

What's GREAT about this?

My personal observation leads me to believe that most people ask the "*why*" of the blame variety. Here's the question I've learned to ask whenever I'm feeling disempowered about any situation — **"WHAT'S GREAT ABOUT THIS?"** When you ask this question, your brain will respond, dive into your memory banks and find the answers. This time though, the answers will make you feel a whole lot more empowered.

My career at IBM went from rock bottom and started its ascendency again the second I consciously chose to reflect on this question. I thought of my one of my colleagues, Su, who had been one of those who took a retrenchment package. She had emailed me and several colleagues shortly thereafter proclaiming she had opened a Thai restaurant in Newtown, inviting all of us to drop in. She shared with us that this had been something she had wanted to do for years. But for many years, she had been one of those that lived on "Someday Isle". "Someday when I have more money, I'll …" "Someday when my children have grown up, I'll ..." "Someday when I've paid off my mortgage, I'll …" She said she was having the time of her life doing what she'd always wanted to do and wished she'd made that decision much earlier.

The restructure and subsequent retrenchment awakened her to the fact that life was too short to procrastinate further. The retrenchment payout provided her with the capital she needed to realise her dream. When I realised that this event had such a positive impact on Su, I instantly felt more empowered about what had happened.

By asking, "What *else* is GREAT about this?", I then thought about Kirk, Glenn, Sunny, Trevor and a host of others who had benefitted from the restructure. They had been more adaptable than most, had embraced the changes and went from being great software architects to exceptional solution architects. In the process they became even more valuable to their team and their clients and opened up more doors of opportunity. I reflected on how the event had really helped the high performers rise to the surface and how much they deserved it for their determination and perseverance.

When I continued to ask, "what *else* is great about this?" I reflected on the small and growing property portfolio I had accumulated in those two years, and how that event had made me realise I had to start learning how to make my money work harder for me, instead of simply working harder for money. The pain of that dark period had driven me to take on what would previously have been considered to me to be "expensive" property investment courses and through application of that knowledge, I had secured several investments that I felt were already putting me in good stead for my future.

I felt a surge of gratitude flow through me. My eyes welled with tears. I realised that I couldn't have taken out bank loans for those investments without the help of having a notable company as my employer. Instantly, I felt my emotions transform from resentment and anxiety to gratitude — not just for my employer but for the situation I had been in.

I realised that I wouldn't have learned about emotional intelligence and been able to apply learnings that were having a positive impact on every aspect of my life if it hadn't been for that incident. This gave me an even deeper sense of inner peace. While for a period there, I must admit I only had unkind thoughts about the manager who had made the call to me that fateful morning, through reflecting on "What's GREAT about this?", I realised that he had been an angel sent to me from above. He was there to gently remind me that I was in my comfort zone and meant to experience and *be* so much more. I shed more tears of appreciation and gratitude.

The event hadn't changed. The meaning I had given to it had. While just a few seconds before I did the exercise I had felt disempowered and bitter, I now only felt profound gratitude.

Choosing Growth and Contribution

The path to resilience and a life of fulfilment is to make our higher order needs for growth and contribution a priority over all else. We each have a strong innate desire to make the lives of others even better through our presence, talents and productivity. However, over time, we humans can allow our environment, upbringing and life experiences to condition ourselves to crave comfort. My parents had seen much suffering and experienced great uncertainty through the second world war. Consciously or otherwise, the people they put on the pedestal as role models of "success" were those who had seemingly comfortable lives. Such folks invariably had overseas tertiary qualifications and drew a good salary that afforded them a comfortable house and all the other creature comforts that were relatively rare back then - air-conditioning, nice furniture, an abundance of food options, a nice car, etc. I never once thought to ask, "How truly *happy and fulfilled* are those people?"

The fact is that humans (and in fact all living creatures in general) are not made to stay in our comfort zones. It's the nature of the human spirit to self-actualise, to crave improvement, to crave progress, to know and be more for ourselves and others around us and to leave a positive, lasting legacy. So whenever we get into our comfort zone, I have learned that the natural order of life is such that events will occur to nudge us out of our comfort zone, to get us into the zone of growth and contribution.

This reminds me of the story of the boy and the cocoon[10]. A young lad who was having a great time playing in his home one day and running in and out of his house, noticed a cocoon perched on the top right hand corner of a doorway. It was vibrating vigorously and he instinctively understood that a struggle of life was occurring. Initially ignoring it, he finally felt compelled to help. Out of the kindness of his heart, he climbed up a stepladder, gently brought the cocoon down and carefully snipped it open with the aid of a pair of scissors. Out popped a beautiful moth. Guess what happened to it? It never learned to fly. The struggle the moth undergoes to get out of its cocoon is nature's way of strengthening its wings. And so it is the same with changes that occur in our lives. They're designed to shake us out of our comfort zone, to remind us that our greatest glory lies beyond the present state and to help us grow in order to realise our highest potential.

Figure 12 - Struggle is nature's way to strengthen our resilience and help us realise our highest potential (Image Credit: Sutisa Kangvansap ©123RF.com)

Today, the constructive "struggle" and willingness I went through during that time of change, to get out of my comfort zone, initiated through asking "What's GREAT about this?" has made me significantly better at public speaking, influence and communication. In turn this has opened up doors that previously were not available. The potential for me to do what I do today was always there, just dormant as I made contentment and my comfort zone a priority. That wake-up call was nature's way of gently reminding me I was capable of being, doing, experiencing, and creating so much more. Truth be told, before the event, I was having a good life, but not a great one.

Learning to embrace growth each and every day, and consciously pushing myself out of my comfort zone to serve a higher purpose, has been one of the most extraordinarily positive life decisions I've made. This has helped me to be far more resilient, achieve more than I could have dreamed, and be far happier than I could have ever imagined possible.

So whenever you're feeling disempowered about any situation, learn to ask, "What's great about this?" This question encompasses other empowering questions like, "What's the opportunity in this situation?" and "What are the positive lessons I can take from it?" (the Curious Why). It is such a powerful force. Just reflecting or meditating on this for several seconds never fails to put me into a state of gratitude. When we're in a state of gratitude, we take even more empowered actions, which generate more positive results. This starts a positive cycle of continuous improvement and success.

Activity

Why don't you do it right now? For a few minutes, just reflect on the following:

- What's GREAT about the situation you're in right now? Write down at least 10 things.

- For each of the things you come up with, ask, "What's great about *that*?"

- Take note of how that makes you feel.

- Go ahead. Press the pause button and do this exercise right now.

So, how was that experience? What emotions came up? Initially, the first range of answers would put you into a more positive state. Did you notice that the more you asked, "What's great" about each response that came up, the more intense the feeling of gratitude became?

This technique is called reframing[11]. To reframe a situation simply means to look at a situation from a different context, angle or "frame". Learning how to reframe a situation in order to create an empowering state change has become one of the most powerful life skills I've learned to be more resilient.

What could be GREAT about this?

"Faith is the bird that sees the light even when the dawn is still dark."

– Rabindranath Tagore

Now, if you're in a situation that you previously decided was terribly negative, don't be surprised if the first answer that comes back when you ask, "What's great about this?" is a raging "Nothing! What could possibly be GREAT about this?" If this is the first instinctive response you get, persist and ask this question instead, "What *could* be great about this?"

You see, what's great about a particular situation is often unclear until sometime later in life. Have you ever in the past labelled a situation as "bad" only to realise later on that what happened actually led to something positive? All of us have stories like this in our life. A relationship gone south that created the space for an even better person to come into your life. A venture that went pear-shaped but subsequently meant we were able to get into something even better. A failure at something that made us even more determined and led to greater success.

[12]Michael Jordan was cut from his varsity basketball team at age 16, missed more than 9,000 shots in his brilliant career, and used the learning from each setback to achieve successes that led to him being considered by many to be the GOAT (Greatest of All Time). Soichiro Honda was turned down by Toyota Motor Corporation for a job after interviewing for a role as an engineer, leaving him jobless for quite some time. He started making scooters of his own at home, spurred on by his neighbours, before finally starting up what today is a multi-billion dollar business employing hundreds of thousands of staff worldwide[13]. Steve Jobs was fired from the company he founded (Apple)[14] and channelled the positive learning from that experience into one of

the most famous comebacks in corporate history, and the world has been so much more enriched through his resilience.

[15]Oprah Winfrey was born out of wedlock to teenage parents who couldn't afford to have her, moved from foster home to foster home, had to abort a pregnancy she herself couldn't afford to have during her teenage years and, for the last decade, has consistently been rated one of the most influential women in the universe. She says, "Be grateful for what you have, and you'll have even more to be grateful for."

When we ask the "Blame Why", there's an underlying pessimistic assumption that this event is a "negative" or "bad" event. Unless you have a crystal ball where you can see everything that would unfold as a result of this event leading right up to the future, why judge the event? An event is only "bad" because we choose to give it that label. My personal observation of optimistic people is that they seem to assume everything that happens is an act of love from nature (or the Universe, God, Yahweh, Allah or another name you use to describe the being that is in charge of the higher order of things), an event that happens *for* them (to serve and help them in some way), rather than to them.

Choosing to be positive is no guarantee of success but it certainly increases your chances and it definitely makes you a whole lot happier. Reflecting on what could be great about any situation you're in is a practical way to act out of faith. Faithful gratitude — the essence of optimism. Here's what I believe - be faithfully grateful and you'll be grateful for your fate!

Forgiveness and Learning to take the Positive Lessons

"Forgiveness is the fragrance that the violet sheds on the heel that has crushed it." — *Mark Twain*

Activity

Is there an event or person in your life that the mere thought of makes you cringe, feel unhappy or disempowered in some way? Something that you're still resentful of?

Take five minutes to reflect on and write down as many answers as you can to the question, "What's been GREAT about that event or person?"

For each response that comes up, ask, "what's been GREAT about that?" Take note of how this makes you feel.

Having come up with a list of positive things, now think about that event or person again. Do you feel the same way or have your feelings towards that event or person changed? Would it be fair to say you feel a whole lot more empowered or grateful for that person or event?

This is a powerful and profound way to let go of latent grudges or resentment. What I love about mastering this reframe is that it takes us beyond acceptance and forgiveness - key traits of highly resilient people - and towards a profound sense of gratitude.

I had a participant in a workshop share her experience with us after completing this exercise.

"When you first asked us to think of a previous event or person that we still harboured resentful feelings towards, the first thing I thought about was that dreadful day six months ago, a week just before my wedding when my fiancée called off our engagement. I still remember being in shock and feeling totally betrayed. For a couple of years since we'd gotten engaged, all we'd spoken about was our desire to start a family. That and my decision to be a full-time mother when we did have kids meant I had put my career on the back-burner, even passing up a couple of career opportunities that had arisen during that time. If that wasn't bad enough, I got home that evening to learn that my mother had been diagnosed of stage 4 cancer. It was the most devastating, gut-wrenching day of my life.

I really thought before I did the exercise that I couldn't possibly find anything positive about such a negative event. But I kept an open mind and did it anyway. To my surprise, by persisting with asking "what's been great about that?" I actually realise now that my life has been so blessed because of that event. Firstly, the break-up meant I could devote all of my attention and energy to helping my mother with her condition. The precious time we've spent together deepened our relationship and mended old wounds. Today, my mum is doing much better than I could have expected. I feel grateful knowing that I was there for her when she needed me most and feel like I have contributed to her recovery. About a month ago, I was offered the dream job of a lifetime, something I would have passed up if I'd gotten married. I accepted it without hesitation and it's been everything I could have ever wished for. Today, my life is so much better because of what happened, not in spite of it. I wish I had done this exercise six months ago instead of harbouring all this resentment this whole time. I feel I have finally let go of this situation. Thank you."

Every change represents a loss of something. As with the law of physics, know that the universe abhors a vacuum. When one is present, something else has to take its place. When you're dwelling on the "Blame Why", you're focussing on what you've lost. Reflecting instead on "What's great about this" helps you connect with what appeared in place of what you've lost. Optimistic people have a knack for doing this. It's what helps them be resilient.

Cultivating an Attitude of Gratitude

> *"Gratitude is not only the greatest of virtues, but a parent of all the others" — Marcus Tullius Cicero*

Imagine what your life would be like if your brain was in fact hardwired with an operating system that goes "What's GREAT about this?" for everything that occurs? How much less stress would you experience? What would your life be like if you were living in a perpetual state of gratitude? How resilient would you be in times of change?

If you want to know the secret to being a model of optimism, positivity, faith and gratitude, it's this — learn to condition your brain to habitually ask the question "What's great about this?", particularly when you're feeling disempowered. The brain is not unlike a hard disc – the more frequently you take time out to reflect on what's great about your life and feel the emotions of gratitude well up, the more this is literally hardwired into your brain. By making this a regular ritual, you're literally reprograming your neural networks from a negativity bias (reinforced by the habit of asking and reacting to the "Blame Why" question) into what "Hardwiring Happiness" author Rick Hanson[16] calls a responsivity bias that helps you stay centred, strong, healthy and happy.

Repeatedly internalising positive experiences builds up inner strengths so you can meet life's challenges without fear, frustration or heartache. Taking in the good reinforces that you are ok right now, that there are always grounds for gratitude and gladness, and that you are cared about and worthy. Over time, your increasingly positive experiences and growing resilience will prevent negative experiences from slipping into your mind and sinking into your brain. Using Hanson's words, "As your mental garden fills with flowers, there's less room for weeds to grow. You'll be sensitizing your brain for the positive, making it a Velcro for good".

For me, the feeling of *gratitude* pretty much beats any other emotion I've experienced in my life. It's a much deeper, more profound emotion than happiness or joy, which can be short-lived. Gratitude makes me feel special, blessed, and it gives me a greater sense of certainty than anything else might. It's the closest feeling I've experienced to fulfilment. Best of all, you get to experience this any time you choose.

Anytime you catch yourself feeling down or disempowered in any way, give yourself the gift of pressing the pause button. Find a quiet spot, close your eyes, and reflect for a few minutes. Again, don't just think but *feel* the answers that arise. Apart from putting you into the most positive state, I've learned the best decisions are made when we're totally in the present, when we're calm and expressing gratitude.

Set aside fixed times every day to practise Mindful Gratitude. I do this first thing every morning and just before I go to sleep. As soon as I wake up, I'll reflect on "what's great about my life right now?" I direct my focus on the smallest things e.g. "I can see", "I can hear", "I am alive", "I have the most beautiful woman in the world whom I feel blessed to call my wife resting right beside me", "I have a comfortable doona", "I have the most wonderful relationship with my three extraordinary children who have been my greatest teachers", "I live in the most wonderful country in the planet, a land of opportunity, where you can create just about anything you set your mind to", "I live in the most extraordinary period in time with access to great technology", "I live in a comfortable home in a lovely suburb", "I have the most wonderful relationship with my parents, brothers, my cousins and their children, Sue's parents and her family each of whom make my life better in some way", "I get to do what I love doing best with and for people I care about and who make my life better", "My future is full of possibilities" … and it makes me feel incredibly humbled and blessed. All this takes maybe a couple of minutes. It's just the most wonderful way to start each day. Every evening before I hit the sack, I'll similarly reflect for a few minutes on "What's been great about today? What have I learned? What's come into my life to make it even better?" This often puts me into a peaceful slumber.

Over the past 15 years, I've studied the lives of people who are optimistic and found a familiar pattern. All of them instinctively ask "What's great about this?' in times of adversity. Two years ago, my niece Rosanne bought me a book called "Will to Live[18]". This book is the re-al-life account of a guy named Matthew, from Brisbane, Australia. About five years ago, Matthew was a regular guy with a lovely wife and four wonderful kids, all under the age of 10. He was a manager at an energy company in Brisbane, a nice guy, popular with friends and colleagues.

One day, Matthew wakes up with flu-like symptoms. Reluctantly, he takes a sickie. A couple of days later, his situation has worsened. Seeing a doctor, he's given a medical certificate and told to rest. Not much can be done, he's told. Just a viral flu.

Almost a week goes by and his situation has deteriorated. Severely dehydrated, he's taken to hospital and put on a drip. Doctors take more tests and finally discover the source of the problem: Streptococcus infection — a life-threatening bacteria.

He's given strong doses of antibiotics, but his situation is so bad and his condition so weak they finally decide to put him into an induced coma. As his body fights on, gangrene creeps in. To save him, they remove an infected limb. Some days later, the doctor calls his wife, siblings and parents into a room. They grimly share their latest prognosis of Matthew's condition. His health is deteriorating so severely they could only see two options – 1: Hope for the best that the medication kicks in (but at the rate of deterioration, he may only have two days to live) or 2: To give him a 1% chance of survival, they would have to amputate all three of his remaining limbs. What would you have done?

Imagine having to make this decision - what attributes of the person lying in bed there would influence your decision? Think about people you have in your life. Would you make the same decision for each of them?

The family deliberated, and after a while, his sister Kate spoke on the family's behalf. "If it was anyone else in this room, we would say let them go. But this is the only person for whom you would do this. This guy is the most pragmatic, positive and calm person you will ever meet. He's an engineer. For him, nothing is ever so big a problem that you can't find a solution."

The surgeons said later that the family's strong conviction and the strength they drew from Matthew's character made them even more determined and confident about succeeding. After the surgery, the battle in Matthew's body continued. Several weeks later, the deterioration stared to plateau and his vital signs started an upward trajectory. Soon, his situation had steadied to the point where the doctors felt comfortable bringing him out of his induced coma. Imagine having to be the person breaking the news to Matthew that day.

Matthew's wife approaches him. He's lying in bed, with a blanket covering the length of his body up to his neck. All he knows is that he has re-gained consciousness but is unable to move. His wife gently recounts every detail of what happened from that fateful day he was brought into the hospital. She looks carefully into his eyes to make sure he understands what she's relaying. And finally, she breaks the news that they had to remove all his limbs just to give him a chance of survival. What do you think his first reaction might have been? In the book, Matthew says that his first thoughts were, "Good decision. I would have made the same call." He goes on to say that he was just grateful that everyone had faith in him. And this next thoughts went to "I have to get home" and then to "I have to find out what I need to do to get better."

Amazing reaction isn't it? Even in a situation most would have de-scribed as soul-destroying, this man found a way to identify it as a blessing. What do you think might have been the question that imme-diately came to his mind when he heard about his situation? I can't be certain but I think it would have been a variation of…

WHAT'S GREAT ABOUT THIS?

And so it is with so many of the people and families I've observed and learned from, who are faced with such significant challenges in their life but are always able to find the positives in their situation.

Having mastered this question, I find these days that hardly anything fazes me. Someone cuts into the lane right in front of me, narrowly missing me. My first thought is "Wow, thanks for keeping me safe. Good luck to you mate. I hope you get where you're going safely." I think maybe, just maybe I've contributed in a small way to this person being able to get to an interview on time, an interview that could just change his life!

I'm stuck in a traffic jam and my first response is "Wow, it's great that I have a nice car, with six-speaker hi-fi stereo and air-conditioning. Far better to be in a traffic jam in Sydney than in Jakarta!" If any of you dear readers have been in Jakarta, and experienced what the locals refer to as "majed" (traffic jam in Bahasa Indonesia), you'll know what I'm talking about! Moreover, when I was a kid growing up in hot and hu-mid Malaysia, there were often seven of us cooped up in a small Morris Minor with no air-conditioning.

When my late Uncle Anthony passed away aged 80, I felt a moment of sorrow, and a sense of loss. A few minutes later, just reflecting on "What's great about this" made me realise how blessed I was that I had 80 years of this wonderful man's life to get to know him. I'd always wished I had gotten to know my paternal grandmother, who had passed on before I was born, at the relatively tender age of 55. I focussed on the large extended family that would be getting together and renewing bonds as we gave this wonderful man a great send-off. And even in that situation, I experienced a deep sense of gratitude and chose to spend those days feeling blessed and celebrating his life rather than feel sorry for myself. Uncle Anthony's passing has indeed brought the entire family closer.

Today, I look forward to catching up with my cousins whenever I travel to Singapore and Malaysia. That event and how we responded to it has indeed strengthened our bonds in a truly special way. And I know that Uncle Anthony would have been proud that his passing has contributed in a very positive way.

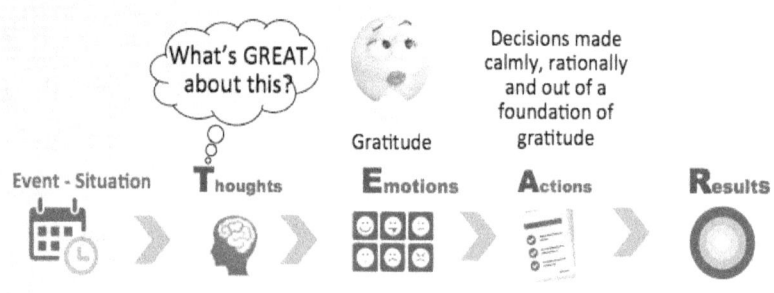

Figure 13 - How asking "What's GREAT about this?" affects our outcomes

So, life will throw lots of things at you. But as the inspirational teacher Brian Tracey[19] says, "It's not how far you fall, it's how high you bounce that matters". What we do with what happens starts off with the questions we ask which drive our focus, how we feel about the situation, what we do, and the outcomes we experience.

This one strategy and habit has certainly been a game-changer for me. Today, my brain is conditioned to ask "What's GREAT about this?" in every situation I may have considered to be negative in the past. Reflecting on the answers makes me feel like the luckiest person on this planet. It makes me feel grateful, blessed, extraordinarily strong, and gives me a deep sense of joy in my heart and a bounce in my step. You deserve to feel that way too!

Action Plan

1. Start a Gratitude Journal. If you're into apps, research and download an app that allows you to write down things you're grateful for in your life. I use an iOS app called Mojo! Take the 10-day Gratitude challenge. Start each morning internalis-ing 10 new things that are going great in your life. Take note of how it makes you feel. Then write that into your Gratitude Journal. Imagine what a great gift that will make for someone one day. After taking the 10-day challenge, see if you can make this part of your daily ritual for the rest of your life!

2. Take a few minutes to reflect on the following:

    - What opportunities are presented by the change you're facing at work?

- Who will benefit from the change? In what way?
- How will your organisation benefit from this change?
- How will the change help you be even better?
- How will the change help others grow?
- How is this change an act of love? By whom?
- What positive lessons can you take from this change?

3. Establish the following ritual – take a few minutes two to three times a day to reflect on the following:

   - What are you proudest of? What makes you feel proud about that?
   - Who do you love? What about them do you love most?
   - What are your greatest strengths? What does it mean to you to have those virtues?
   - What are you most excited about?
   - What inspires you?

CHAPTER 8

How Resilient People Act

"People are always blaming their circumstances for what they are. I don't believe in circumstances. The people who get on in this world are the people who get up and look for the circumstances they want, and, if they can't find them, make them." — George Bernard Shaw

Success Strategies of the Highly Resilient

"**Strategy** without tactics is the slowest route to victory. Tactics without **strategy** is the noise before defeat." — Sun Tzu

Being in a state of gratitude is a great foundation for deciding what you'd like your future outcomes to be. But to thrive through change, you must not stop at feeling optimistic. Winners live by the philosophy of not being dissatisfied by their lot, while at the same time remaining *unsatisfied*. They believe in turning "lemons" into lemonade by firstly defining the ideal outcomes they want from the situation, understanding how achieving those outcomes will benefit them and those around them and then using the pursuit of these ideal outcomes as an opportunity to grow and learn. Once they're clear about their desired outcomes, they decide to take massive action towards making it a reality.

Having studied the way winners think for the last 15 years, I've learned that they all apply a similar strategy or pattern of behaviour during times of change:

1. **Start with Gratitude** — reflect on "What's great about where I am right now?"

2. **De ine a Vision** of your ideal future — ask, "What do I really want?"

3. **Internalise your Purpose** — reflect on "Why is achieving this a must for me? Who will benefit from my achieving these outcomes? How will it benefit me and others around me?"

4. **Take courageous Action** — ask and act on, "What will I do?"

5. **Review, Improve and Adapt** — proactively find ways to make it even better

   - Review what you're getting — ask "On a scale of 1 – 10, where am I relative to my goal? How am I doing with the effort and quality of the effort I am putting in?"

   - Celebrate what's working — ask, "What's working?"

   - Learn from what's not — ask, "What can I do even better?"

   - Adapt your strategy if required and get back to Step 4.

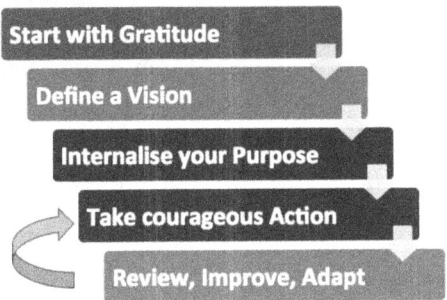

Figure 14 - Success strategy of the Resilient

Exercise your personal leadership

Paul Meyer defines personal leadership as: *"The self-confident ability to crystallise your thinking so that you are able to establish an exact direction for your own life; to commit to yourself to moving to that direction and then to take committed action to acquire, accomplish or become whatever that goal demands."*

When it comes to dealing with change, whiners are reactive, allowing the twin forces of pain and pleasure to drive their behaviour. They're like boats without a specific destination that they're committed to, shifting direction depending on the direction of the wind or the storm. Without a clear vision of an ideal, desired outcome, the human brain focuses on survival and comfort, making decisions based on what's least painful or most pleasurable. Very often, the storms in their life are so violent that the boat capsizes and through mighty stress and effort, they finally get the ship upright, only for the next big storm to turn it over again. The boat's sail gets torn and tattered; it often lists aimlessly getting occasionally excited at the sight of shelter and food. After a while, these people become so dejected they start giving up on life.

And then there are folks like Jessica Watson[1], who at the age of 16, became the youngest ever to sail around the globe unassisted. I remember waking up around 9am on the 15th of May, 2010. I turned on the telly and it was showing a teenage girl on a boat, making her way into Sydney Harbour. I changed the channel, same picture. And each of the next three free-to-air channels were the same. I thought for a moment that the remote control wasn't working until I realised that I was witnessing a truly historic moment live. The foreshores of Sydney Harbour were lined with thousands of people, all who had braved the early morning and gathered to watch Jessica Watson's historic homecoming. Her successful return would make an entry to the Guinness Book of World Records that day.

As the story unfolded and we watched Jessica patiently and skilfully make her way through the turbulent waters of Sydney Heads, I listened to interviews of many who had gone out there to watch. The responses weaved a similar thread "She's my idol. I can't believe she's made it happen. Her courage inspires me so much. I couldn't ever imagine being able to achieve what she's achieved." Here was a girl who had defied all odds and naysayers. Many had tried to discourage her from her journey, saying it was far too treacherous for someone of such a tender age. Even her parents had been publicly criticised. In spite of all the negativity, this girl was resolute in her determination to complete what she felt was an important part of her life journey.

When I read more about her journey, I learned that at least three times through her voyage, violent storms and weather had turned her boat upside down. She had periods where she was in the water, hanging on to the side of the boat for dear life for hours on end, just patiently waiting for the storm and weather to subside. Each time it did, she would do whatever it took to get the boat upright, set her destination and charge forward again. **Could you imagine her starting her journey without absolute clarity over her desired destination and the timing she would take to get there?**

That's what winners do. The same storm blows on all of us, but winners know where they end up is a matter of how they set the sail. And set the sail they do, towards a definite, specific destination they'd set before starting the journey.

Defining a Vision

"If you don't know where you're going, any road will take you there"
— Alice in Wonderland

There are two reasons for always setting goals, and being clear about your ideal vision. Firstly, having a clear sense of direction gives you a feeling of certainty, something we all need during times of change when it's easy to feel like we're losing control of the situation.

Back in 2001, if you had asked me "Where do you see yourself in five years?", I'd have said, "I have no idea." This was contributing to my uncertainty and to my personal stress levels. I wish I knew then what I know now. Today, whenever people who are undergoing change come to me with the question, "What should I do? I have been offered Option

A and Option B", I always ask them "Where do you ideally see yourself one, two, three years from today?" To which they often reply, "I don't know." My response is always the same, "if that's the case, then choose either one. It doesn't matter. Either option will take you there."

It's the same with the 90% of the cabbies I come across who feel overwhelmed by the transformation taking place in their industry. Whenever I ask them, "Where do you see yourself a year from today?", the response is predictably similar, "One year? I don't even know where I'll be in one week let alone 12 months." I had one particular cabbie really reflect on this for a few moments. I still remember seeing his eyeballs first moving upwards, sideways, and then downwards as he desperately sought an answer. Finally, he turned to me with a perplexed look and said, "Is that important?" I simply smiled and said "Imagine when I got into your cab five minutes ago and you asked me where I'd like to go and my response was "I don't know. Is that important?" I wonder where you would take me. The surest way to get nowhere is by not having a goal." If your managers haven't clearly communicated a path forward, take the initiative and ask them. Show them you have initiative and leadership. Project curiosity, positivity and confidence. Don't be surprised if you don't get a clear response. Often, they themselves are coming to terms with having to lead and plan a change that was initiated from above them. If there's one thing we can safely assume about people and managers, they're not the best communicators. Most simply haven't been taught the skills of empathy and the art of creating and communicating a clear vision during times of uncertainty. At other times, they may have communicated that a change is happening but need more time to work out and get senior alignment on the clear path forward. Don't be disheartened by this.

Take charge of setting up a clear path for yourself, using whatever information you have and tapping into your intuition and imagination. This is what exercising your personal leadership is all about. You want to be a leader that your inner soul is prepared and inspired to follow. Know that you can always change course later as more information emerges. The key thing is to chart your ideal path and once you have done so, start moving forward with positivity and enthusiasm, focussing on the journey (as opposed to the destination) and seeing it as a growth and development opportunity for you.

Activity

Let's do this now. Take a deep breath in and focus all your attention firstly on your breathing for several seconds.

Now place both hands over your heart and focus on the beating of your heart for several seconds.

Close your eyes and think of something that you're truly grateful for. It could be as simple as the beating of your heart, something we take for granted, but which gives you the strength and vitality and the gift of life to enjoy all that's good in your life.

Think of something else that's great in your life. Take another deep breath in and feel the sense of gratitude well up from within.

Now I'd like you to imagine floating to a time in the future, say six months from today. Think about your ideal career situation. If anything were possible, what would your ideal position be? Would you still be in your organisation? If so, what would your role involve? Who would you ideally be reporting to? How many people would be reporting in to you? If your ideal role is outside your present organisation, what would that organisation be? Would you be self-employed or working for another organisation? What would your role be? Who are your customers or people benefitting from the value you create? Who would you be working with? In what way are they benefitting from your efforts? What would your ideal level of remuneration be six months from today?

Think about the ideal state of your relationships with your manager and colleagues. If anything were possible, six months from today, what would that be like?

If anything were possible, what would the state of your health, vitality, energy and stress levels be like?

How would you ideally like to feel? What emotional states would your life be predominantly filled with?

Think about the quality of relationship you'd like to have with your family and friends six months from today. What would you ideally like those relationships to be like?

What about the hobbies and other passions you have in your life? If anything were possible, what other goals would you like to have ticked off so you could say that these six months were the most extraordinary months of your life?

Think of the ideal person you'd like to become in the next six months. How have you grown? What's your level of knowledge, competence, creativity, enthusiasm, confidence and passion like?

Now open your eyes and write down or draw everything you visualised. Don't be afraid of making mistakes or strive too much for perfection at this stage. Your goal is simply to put into words, pictures or symbols what you saw, heard or felt that you'd like to achieve. Go ahead and do that right now.

Well done! Read back what you've written down. Now, project yourself again into the future six months from today. Imagine having achieved the ideal outcomes you defined above. How does this make you feel?

What emotions came up? Are you feeling more inspired or motivated? Feeling more confident and at peace?

Isn't it great to know that you can turn on these emotional states simply by imagining yourself already achieving your goals? Again, know that you can create these states any time you wish simply by tapping into one of your greatest gifts – your imagination. During times of change, we all need the certainty that comes from having a clear sense of direction. Know that everything great that was ever created – the room you're in, the country you live in, the family you have — was once but a figment of someone's imagination. The regular use of this creativity and imagination is a trait that distinguishes winners from whiners. It's what makes you a leader in the eyes of others and hopefully, through this process, strengthens your conviction to follow the leader in you!

The second benefit of defining your preferred outcomes in advance is that it provides you with a shot of inspiration, something we all need during times of change. And best of all, you have full control over this process. Regardless of what your external environment may be, all the resources you need to chart your path and create the emotional drive to propel you forward are already within you. Doesn't that make you feel a lot more empowered?

When I did this exercise, I decided I wanted to help turn my team into one that was even more resilient, dynamic and positive. I saw a team that wasn't just hitting its straps and reaching our new organisational goals, but one that was united, determined, and positive in its quest. I imagined myself developing a deeper understanding of my new role and contributing effectively and to the best of my ability to make my team and I a success — achievements that would give us a deep sense of satisfaction. I saw that by leading by example, I was also empowering my managers with the skills to lead and manage change even more effectively. And finally, I visualised myself becoming a more inspirational leader and coach for my team. I saw myself as not only being proficient with the operational aspects of the business but also as the ultimate cheerleader and coach for my team.

Just focussing on achieving this made me feel inspired. I felt a renewed sense of purpose and optimism. I was charged up and ready to break through barriers.

Internalise your Purpose

"You have power over your mind, not outside events. Realise this and you will find strength."

— Marcus Aurelius

"If your why is big enough, the how will work itself out."

Having a clear, exciting and inspiring vision is great, but it's just the start. Step 3 in the success strategy is to connect emotionally with *why* achieving that vision is important to you. We've spoken about not using the "Blame Why" and tapping into the "Curious Why". This third "why" is another I encourage you to reflect on often. I call it the "Purpose Why".

"Great leaders", Simon Sinek[2] says, "start with the *Why?*"

The bigger and bolder your vision, the larger the obstacles you can expect to face. The actions you'll need to take to achieve your vision are likely to be significantly outside your comfort zone. Fear and doubt can creep in to extinguish the flames of your imagination, and whether or not you'll follow through to take the action necessary to turn your vision into reality will boil down to one thing: *how badly do you want it?* Having a strong purpose will give you the inner drive and motivation to overcome fear and break through the seemingly insurmountable obstacles that may arise along your journey.

Just as we don't complain about gravity but instead find ways to tap into its power, use your understanding that humans are intrinsically driven by the need to avoid pain and gain pleasure to create both inner push and pull factors to drive you towards your vision. By internalising your "Purpose Why", you are in essence using the deep sense of intrinsic pain you create about your status quo (the "push") and the unquenchable desire to experience the pleasure of your ideal future state ("pull") to propel you forward towards your vision.

The Importance of Internalising a Compelling "Purpose"

Throughout my coaching journey, I've met many people who *do* have clear goals but who fail to follow through. The reasons they give are almost always a variation of "I can't", "too old", "too young", "not enough money", "no time", "not the right gender", "not smart enough", "not the right qualifications", etc. or they point to how their "children are too young", and the "timing's not right" somehow. Based on my experience, having seen the seemingly impossible achieved by who you and I would consider ordinary mortals, the real difference is the level of passion, motivation or hunger to achieve whatever you set out to achieve. When people say, "I can't", what they often really mean is, "I haven't made this important enough". This is often a reflection that they're valuing comfort and security more than growth and contribution.

I give them the following example. "Imagine you're standing on one side of a six-lane freeway. Cars are zipping past, back and forth, fast. In fact, imagine the cars going at speeds in excess of 200 km/hr, just like on the autobahns in Germany. I say to you — visualise — see yourself on the other side of the freeway. Now, I want you to get across in 10 seconds. Will you do it?"

Predictably, they shake their heads. I then ask "why not?" And they'd say, "Why would I endanger my life like that?" To which I say, "How about if I gave you 50 bucks? Would you do it?" Again, they'd shake their heads. "No way!" I'd continue to increase the stakes offering $100, then $1,000, $10,000, etc. Often, I'd get to the millions and still have some people resolutely saying "no". When asked why, they'd invariably say, "My life's worth much more than that!" I had a guy in Singapore, where people are generally more risk-adverse say, "Don't waste your breath. What's the use of the money if I'm dead?"

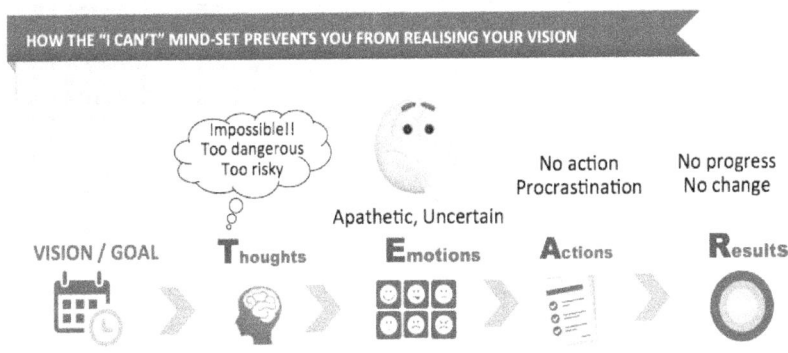

Figure 15 – How the "I CAN'T" mindset prevents you from realising your vision

And then I'd say, "Apart from you, who's the most important person in your life?" The response is typically a family member — a child, spouse or parent. "Imagine that person (child, parent, partner, friend) on the other side of the freeway. He or she is excitedly coming towards you and for some reason does not realise the danger. You're screaming at the top of your lungs for them to stay where they are. They can't hear you through the din of the traffic. Unless you're across in 10 seconds, their life would be in mortal danger. Will you run across to save them?"

Without a second's hesitation, they'd say, "Yes". The impossible just became possible.

If this situation were to arise in real life, would you not only think they will cross but do this successfully?

Chances are, they will. Sadly, most humans only discover how truly capable they are when they're backed into a corner. Throughout my journey, I've been inspired by so many who've reached great heights from seemingly desperate situations. Have you heard or read about cancer patients who were only given months to live and who not only survived but turned their lives around to live an even fuller and more enriching life than before they had cancer? Or how about the guy who was born without hands and legs, who at age eight almost ended his life and subsequently became an inspirational speaker, touching the lives of millions around the world (Nick Vujicic[3])? Have you watched the real life drama or read the story of the adventure enthusiast who found himself in dire straits trapped all alone in a canyon in the desert after a 500 kg rock had come crashing down to smash his right hand and trap it against the canyon wall? In his greatest moment of desperation, he amputated his right hand with a pocket knife to free himself, lowered himself 20 metres to the ground and walked 10 kms to his car to save himself — after six days without food and only two litres of water (Aaron Ralston[4]).

Each of them shared something in common; a clear vision of what they wanted to achieve and a deep hunger for success that made achieving that vision a MUST! Each was driven by a clear and compelling purpose.

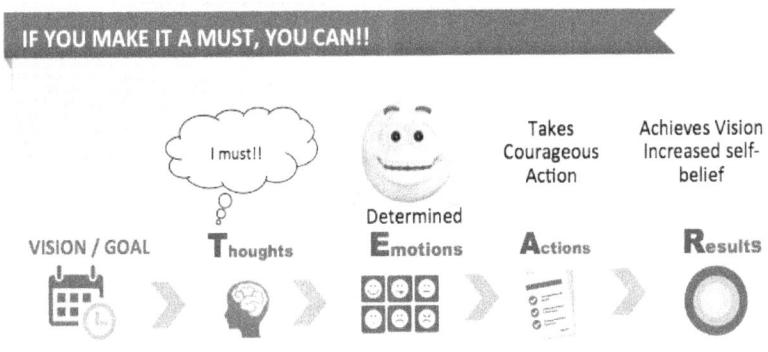

Figure 16 - **If you make it a MUST, you CAN!!**

Our biggest barriers to our highest potential and fulfilment in life, often lies within us. We have an addiction to comfort and fearing what we could lose, rather than focussing on what we stand to gain. Barriers are also due to poor strategies or the lack of discipline to follow the success steps in the right sequence. Setting a goal and then jumping right into taking action is like setting your GPS to direct you to the top of the mountain but not ensuring your car has the right fuel or horsepower for the climb. Do not skip Step 3 of the Success Strategy, internalising a strong and compelling purpose. Each step of the strategy is important and it's equally essential that you follow the right sequence. A strategy is not unlike a recipe to bake a great cake. You may pick up a recipe used by the best chefs in the world, but if you were to put the batter into the oven without first heating the oven for a period of time or forget to sift the flour, chances are your cake will not turn out as you'd expect!

Balance risk with benefits

Achieving a vision is something you'll never be able to do simply by thinking rationally and finding a logical solution. It's just unavoidable that too often, the rational part of our brain hijacks this process by saying "You've never done something like that before so it's unlikely you'll achieve it now."

Due to the negativity bias our brain has formed over many years, we tend to exaggerate the probability and negative consequences of the worst-case scenarios and underestimate the probability and positive benefits of the likely and best-case scenarios.

Take the vision you've created for instance and reflect on the following:

- On a scale of 1 to 10, what's the likelihood of you failing?

- On a scale of 1 to 10, what's the impact of failure? Who would be impacted? How much would that set you back by? In what way?

- In the journey to realising your vision, how would you benefit? Who would benefit? How would your life be changed if you were to achieve that?

- So what will you do today to propel yourself forward?

In my case, I learned the worst thing that could happen in my journey of transforming myself and my team, was that I would take invaluable lessons on how I could improve my personal leadership and influence skills, endure some possibly unflattering remarks and in the process, develop a thicker skin.

On the other hand, the upside of success was tremendous and possibly life changing. Not only would I get the deep sense of pride and satisfaction of knowing I had made a difference to my colleagues, but the opportunities and doors that could open up from this would be enormous. I would be even more excited and optimistic about my future and learn tremendous skills in the process.

Doing this made me feel even more confident and determined to go ahead with my plan!

Tap into your higher need to Serve

To get the most mileage from tapping into your "Purpose Why", remember that all of us are born with an innate need to contribute to a higher purpose, and that we're often willing to do far more for those we care about than we are for ourselves. In the previous example of crossing the freeway, many say it's impossible even when the financial reward would benefit them personally and in a significant way. However, when it came to saving those we care about, I have not had one person hesitate to say, "Yes, I will and yes, I can!"

When you internalise your why, be sure to reflect on how *others* around you and those you most care about, are adversely affected physically, emotionally, mentally and spiritually by the status quo, and how they'd also benefit from you achieving your vision.

To tap into this powerful source of intrinsic motivation called purpose, learn to reflect on the following:

Imagine if one year from now, the high levels of stress and uncertainty you're experiencing remain unchanged, how much more pressure would build up?

Who else would suffer from the negative consequences? In what way?

What are the ultimate consequences to your family, health, finances, self-belief and self-confidence, on opportunities missed if the status quo remained unchanged?

Now imagine achieving that vision. Who would benefit? In what way? Write down as many people and benefits as you can.

How would they benefit? How would that make you feel?

This exercise had a very profound impact on me. The status quo had affected my levels of energy, passion and confidence and was having a negative impact not just on me but also on others around me. I thought of my colleagues and staff that I'd let down by being the "absent leader" during those turbulent times. I reflected on all those lost, precious moments with my family when I was physically present but emotionally, spiritually, and mentally absent, wallowing in self-pity, guilt, and resentment. I reflected on the negative impact the status quo had on my self-esteem and self-confidence, and on the layers of guilt weighing me down. I realised I had been having regular bouts of the flu and that the high levels of stress would have contributed to a weakened immune system that in the long term could result in grave consequences.

On the other hand, just reflecting on how my life would be when I'd achieved my vision brought a tremendous surge of excitement through my veins. I started to feel really alive and abuzz again - nervous but excited. Something that I hadn't felt in a long time. I thought of my children and saw how proud they would be of me one day, when I could tell them I personally transformed myself and went from being that nerdy geek to a professional speaker and coach. I saw the positive impact my actions could have on them, paving their path ahead to do what they loved doing best, because I had been a great role model for them.

I imagined how the level of my attention and positive presence that comes from being truly alive and passionate about life would translate into a more intimate relationship with my wife. By doing what truly inspired me, I would have great anecdotes to share with her. Being someone who had shared in my journey of highs and lows, I saw my personal transformation also inspiring her and helping her be even more confident about pursuing all that she was passionate about. And that made me feel deeply content.

I imagined how proud my parents would feel to see their son find his wings and truly soar, knowing they had contributed much to my well-being. I saw how my joy and success would have a positive impact on my brothers and my extended family through my courage to listen to my inner voice and be different.

I saw the faces of my team, who'd start finding even more energy and joy in the workplace and through what they did. The thought of my team being a role model for the rest of the organisation in thriving through challenging moments motivated me.

I saw the faceless strangers of each of my workshop participants and coaches, readers of my book, whose lives were positively impacted by my courage and willingness to share my personal journey. Yes, whether or not you realise it, *you* were part of the reason that compelled me to push forward with determination. I have you to thank for contributing to the exceptional life I'm privileged to have.

So dear friend, know that the process of setting a goal is incomplete without reflecting on and writing down a strong and compelling why. Tap deeply into this rich vein of infinite resource called passion that you already have in you – the love you have for others – to enrich your why and deepen your commitment to your cause.

Figure 17 - With passion that comes from your well of Purpose, the impossible becomes possible (Image Credit: gajus ©123RF.com)

The vision gives you a clear sense of direction. Your purpose will be the invisible tool you'll tap into again and again to make possible the impossible.

The Purpose-Driven Cabbie

During my impromptu "coaching" sessions with my poor, unsuspecting taxi drivers, two staple questions I use to help them tap into their intrinsic sources of motivation are firstly, "Where do you see yourself in 12 months?" (Vision) and then "Why do you do what you do?" (Purpose). The ones who feel overwhelmed by change typically have no long-range goals. Their answer to the latter is typically along the lines of "I have no choice. I have bills to pay". How inspired would you be to get out of bed every day when your key purpose was to "pay the bills"? Predictably, the level of service you get from such cabbies is invariably average, the cars are often not the cleanest and they often don't smell great.

[5]About 20% of the people in every role in every organisation are the "stars" — the high performers who stand out with their energy, commitment, passion and quality of execution. These 20% typically deliver 60-80% of the team's results. And so it is with cabbies. I have also been blessed to encounter many of these 20 percenters who are the shining lights of their industry. They are models of exemplary, cheery service who go above and beyond the call of duty to deliver a memorable experience for their customers each and every day.

One such individual was a gentleman named Suria from Kuala Lumpur (KL). About eight years ago, Sue and I were in downtown KL to facilitate a program to help a client groom selected high potential managers for senior roles. After another high energy and spiritually fulfilling day, we headed out to the taxi rank just outside our client's premises to hail a cab. It was around 5:30 pm and a typically hot and humid day in Malaysia. We had a 9:30 pm flight to catch that evening and had been forewarned that it would take a good 90 to 120 minutes during that time of day to get to KLIA (Kuala Lumpur International Airport). Above the din and cacophony of the infamous KL peak-hour traffic, I felt reasonably confident that we would get to the airport with time to spare. Feeling exhausted as I always do after giving my all that day, and with my suit on in hot and humid Malaysia, I was feeling distinctly uncomfortable and could feel the beads of sweat forming little streams that ran down my back, causing my soaked shirt to cling to my skin. I couldn't wait to get into a cab, hopefully one with decent air-conditioning.

The first taxi arrived. Mr Cabbie wound down the front passenger seat window and said, in a typical Malaysian accent, "Where you off to sir?" "KLIA!", I said with great enthusiasm. To my surprise, all I got was a terse "Sorry sir. Cannot-lah! Traffic jam. Find another taxi!" and Mr Cabbie just drove off in a huff! I couldn't imagine a cabbie in Sydney turning down a trip – let alone one with a carrot of a decent 1.5hr ride! Next cabbie, same story. And so it was with the third and fourth. By this time, my initial optimism of getting to the airport on time was starting to ebb. Through my brief exchanges with the unobliging cabbies, I'd worked out that in Malaysia, the meter slows down when the taxi slows down. This conditions them to firstly always be on top of what the traffic conditions are like and secondly to favour rides to places that weren't clogged traffic-wise.

Cabbie number five pulled up and greeted us with a cheery "Where to sir?" Hearing my tentative "KLIA?", he replied with the same enthusiasm "No problems sir. Just one condition, sir. I turn off the meter and we agree on the price before we go. Is that ok, sir?" I breathed a sigh of relief. Finally, a cabbie that was offering me options! "Sure!" I said, matching his enthusiasm. "How much?" "100 ringgit sir!" Now that was the first time I'd ever taken a taxi for that length of distance in KL and so I had no idea if that was the right price. But to an Aussie, 100 ringgit is about AUD35.00 - quite inexpensive for a 90-minute ride back home. So I said without hesitation, "You're on!! Thank you."

On this occasion, I hopped into the back seat. My head was throbbing both from physical and mental exhaustion, as well as the heat. I felt ever so grateful for the cool breeze of the air-conditioner and the pleasant scent of the air freshener in the car. All I wanted to do then was to shut my eyes and just tune out for a while. I nudged Sue and said, "Why don't you do the coaching this time?"

With most cabbies, I'm usually the one to initiate a conversation. With this guy, it was just the opposite. You couldn't shut him up! "Where are you from sir?" I looked up and our eyes connected in the rear view mirror. I was impressed by his enthusiasm and cheery nature. If only we had more cabbies with personalities!! "Sydney", I said. "But I actually grew up not far from here. Seremban, 40 miles south to be exact. Can't you tell?" He said, "Sir, I can tell you have been away for a long time. You're different to the typical Malaysian." "Well, I hope that's not a bad thing. I'll take that as a compliment", I said. "You come here often?" he asked. I told him that I did, that I was a consultant with clients in Malaysia and that I particularly loved travelling to Malaysia as it gave me the opportunity to drop in on my parents who still lived in Seremban. He asked me which parts of Malaysia I travelled to and I shared with him that I had clients in Kuala Lumpur, Malacca, Johor Baru and also neighbouring Singapore.

"Sir, sit back and relax. Bumper-to-bumper traffic, sir, but don't you worry. I know what time your flight is. I'll get you there safely and on time."

I breathed a sigh of relief. That was so reassuring. "A cabbie with a decent EQ – such a different experience", I thought.

He went on, "Sir, would you prefer to take a nap or if you like, I can tell you a joke?" Now, in all my years of taking cabs, that was the first time I'd ever had a cabbie offer me a joke. So, much as I would have had preferred at that moment to just have some shut-eye, I did not have the heart to dampen his enthusiasm. "Sure!" I said. He told me a joke and we both cracked up. Five jokes later, he said "You like my jokes sir?" I remember being so impressed at his energy and complimented him on this. I told him that in all my years of taking taxis, his level of service really stood out and that he would be a person anyone would want in their team. He thanked me for the compliment and said he had 100 jokes up his sleeve which he had practised over the years to keep his guests entertained, anticipating long dreary rides in bumper-to-bumper traffic — it was his strategy to keep himself and his guests energised.

I learned that he loved driving because it gave him a lot of flexibility. Impressed by his positive attitude, I asked him where he ideally saw himself in five years.

Without batting an eye-lid, he replied, "Five years? Oh that's easy. Five years from now sir, my family and I, we'll be in the UK sir."

Surprised and impressed at the clarity and boldness of his vision, I asked him what he'd be doing in the UK.

"Working as a nurse in a nursing home sir", he replied with just as much conviction.

Now, in Malaysia at that time, the culture was such that it was still relatively uncommon for blokes to choose nursing as a career, let alone choose to work in a nursing home. Nursing homes in Malaysia are generally for the elderly with a lower socio-economic background or those who did not have families who could look after them. They are typically run by non-profit organisations with a religious bent e.g. the Little Sisters of the Poor. The social expectation of the culture is that children are to look after their parents in the twilight of their years. And so out of curiosity I decided to probe his "Purpose Why". "So why nursing and why a nursing home?"

He said, "Best job in the world sir. It's so fulfilling being able to help those who often can't help themselves. You feed them, help them put their clothes on and they thank you again and again. Some of these people, their children don't even visit them."

He told me that he was a qualified nurse and had previously spent quite a few years working in a nursing home in the UK, something he really enjoyed. Quite apart from it being a fulfilling vocation, the strength of the UK pound relative to the Malaysian ringgit meant that it was also financially rewarding. At the time he had three young children living back in Malaysia under the care of his wife, and everything had been going very smoothly until he received a fateful call from his eldest son one day. His son (then 12 years old and in the 6th year of primary school) asked him when he'd be coming home, and said that he hadn't seen his dad for some 18 months and he missed him. Suria learned from this wife that his son was being bullied in school, was really struggling academically and that she was worried about how he'd perform in the national Year 6 examinations that year.

In the Malaysian education system, the student's results in this particular test, called the Primary School Achievement Test (or "Ujian Pen-capaian Sekolah Rendah" in Malay) has a significant bearing on one's options for secondary schooling. He told his son that he needed him to truly focus on his studies and promised him that he would return to Malaysia if his son scored five As in that exam. His son simply listened with silence and hung up the phone.

After a few months, he received another phone call from his son. "When are you coming home Papa? I scored five As! You said if I scored five As, you'd come home. Have you bought your air ticket?" He told me he was caught off guard, that it was a tremendous surprise and that he felt a deep sense of joy and pride and yet guilt as he felt he couldn't fulfil the promise he had made to his son. He tried to explain to his son that such decisions were not easy ones to make but that his son was deeply unhappy with his response, accused him of not being a man of his word and hung up the phone. He told me that he walked around all day with a heavy heart, unable to concentrate on his job. He felt confused — his thinking brain told him he was doing the right thing by his family and yet his emotional brain caused him to feel only guilt and fear, of losing a relationship that he treasured so much.

Finally, he could take it no longer and approached his manager for a coaching moment. His manager was a wise and empathetic man. Suria explained his predicament and as the man listened intently, he asked him for his counsel. "Tell me what I should do", he said.

His manager said that there was no right or wrong answer to life's predicaments like this. And that it boiled down to being congruent to one's innermost values. He said that all he could do for him was to offer him a question to reflect on, and made him promise that he would base his decision on the first intuitive response that came up, to listen to his inner voice, which was "always right". When asked what the question was, his manager said, "Imagine I were a doctor and I came to you and said "Suria, I'm sorry to break the bad news to you but I'm afraid you only have six months to live." What would you do? Would you stay here and look after these wonderful old folks or would you go back to your family?"

"And so you see sir, I'm back here driving a taxi because that day, by reflecting on that great question, I realised what was most important to me at that point of my life. I did not want to miss out on being part of the precious growing up phase of my children's life and so I decided to come home. My goal was to spend as much time as I could with my children. I needed a job that would give me flexibility and that would help me sustain a decent lifestyle at least for the next five years. The nursing homes in Malaysia do not offer the same opportunities as in the UK and so I decided to drive a cab. This job is amazing sir. I get to drop my kids off to school, pick them up and if you're smart, the money's actually not bad, sir. In five years, my family will be ready to move with me to the UK. I have a job waiting there for me."

I was so inspired by this wonderful man's story. I thought I was being the coach that day, but instead, I got coached. It reminded me that whatever situation you face in your life, if you have a clear vision of what you'd like to achieve and connect with your deepest why, how you get there will work itself out. I said to him "Thank you for sharing such a wonderful story with me. You are a wonderful human being. I will always remember you."

At that moment, we arrived at our destination. He turned to me and said, "Sir. I hope you have enjoyed this ride. I have really enjoyed our conversation. By the way, how do you find my car? Is it clean?" I said, "Yes, in fact it is spotless." He then said, "Does it smell good?" I nodded my approval. "It's so important to me that my passengers enjoy their ride. That's why I look after every detail, including making sure the car smells right." He then reached out to his glove box, opened it up and pulled out a business card. I remember thinking what a novelty that the cabbie has a business card! He said, "Sir. No obligations but next time you come to Malaysia or Singapore, if you'd like for me to pick you up at the airport, I'd be delighted to do that for you. Just give me a call 24 hours beforehand. We agree on a fixed price and I'll be waiting for you." He showed me a stack of business cards bound together by a rubber band and shared with me that he had regular clients from all over the world who loved his service and reliability. And that every day of the week, he could count on between two to four airport pickups or drop-offs which he really valued and enjoyed.

Now do you think I'll remember this cabbie? You bet! What an exceptional individual. So let's take two cabbies, both working in the same environment. One is stressed and feels totally disempowered in the face of relentless change. The other is thriving on it. One says his or her daily takings depend on luck and the weather. The other makes his own luck. And the quality of the service and the experience you get with both cabbies is like chalk and cheese. More importantly, which cabbie do you think is having more fun? What's the difference? It has nothing to do with their driving competencies, or knowledge of the roads. Those are important of course, but the key differentiator is their resilience, adaptability, optimism and emotional intelligence – the way they choose to think, feel and act in every situation. One has a clear vision and compelling purpose, sees his job as a stepping stone to his dreams, and feels blessed about it. Faced with adversity, his strong why pushes him to tap into his resourcefulness, focussing on solving the problem and finding answers to "how can I?" The other sees his job just as a means to pay the bills, lacks an inspiring vision and compelling purpose and ends up focussing on the problem and all the reasons why he can't, blaming the environment in the process.

Take Courageous Action

> *"Change is hard at first, messy in the middle, and gorgeous at the end."* — Robin Sharma

Armed with a clear vision and compelling purpose, the next step in the Success Strategy is to formulate an action plan and take courageous, constructive action towards your goal. In times of uncertainty, it's normal to feel paralysed with fear and doubt, and tempting to play the "wait and see" game. Know that the best way to feel confident and positive is to act decisively like someone who is. Remember that courage is not the absence of fear, but the decision to make something else more important than fear. Heed the words of Mark Twain, who says, "Do the thing you fear most and the death of fear is certain[6]". Taking action enables you to utilise your skills, talents and energy to make a difference to others, which also strengthens your self-esteem.

By being valuable to others, you increase opportunities that come your way. Remember that your managers are also humans — they're attracted to people who are energy-givers. Many more opportunities will come to you when you project that positive energy and initiative. The attitude that says, "I can't change the change, but I can use every opportunity presented during these times to learn all I can and contribute the best way I can to keep the business going and at the same time, develop valuable skills, experiences, and relationships that will get me to where I'd like to be."

Every week, set aside a quiet hour to review your vision and purpose, celebrate your wins for the week and set goals for the next week that will take you constructively forward towards turning the vision into reality.

Every evening before getting into bed or just before heading home from work, review your journey and successes of the day, celebrate every little win you've had (including precious lessons learned) and, after tapping into your emotional well of gratitude and inspiration, set goals for the next day by devoting some time focussing on answering this question:

"If tomorrow were my last day at my workplace, what would I do to make the biggest, most positive and meaningful difference to my colleagues and family around me and in a way that will move me towards my vision?"

Building Resourcefulness

If you're stuck for ideas about what you could do, instead of deciding that you can't, focus your entire energies into finding answers. Learn to develop a "how can I?" mindset. Brainstorm at least 20 answers to the following questions:

1. What resources (knowledge, skills, strategies, tools, money, a better CV, testimonials, opportunities, systems, people, contacts, ideas, energy, etc.) do I need that could help me get to my outcome?

2. What could I do to get the resources I need?

3. What will I do today?

In brainstorming steps 1 to 3 above, remember **not** to judge the ideas that come up but to get a flow of ideas. Part of the value of this process is to create certainty for yourself. The more options you have, the more certain you feel about your path forward. Don't stop until you come up with 20 answers. This will really stretch you but resourcefulness is a muscle you need to build. Be creative.

Tapping into the resources of others

Any problem you're facing, remember that chances are someone has already solved it. Don't hesitate to tap into the knowledge and experience of others. By all means, involve others in the brainstorming process above. Don't be afraid to seek help. Get a mentor or coach. Remember that people find it fulfilling to help so you're also doing them a favour. The main thing to remember when you seek help is to genuinely be open to ideas and if you find something worthwhile, be sure to give it a go and close the loop off with your mentor or coach to tell them about what you've done and the results you've achieved. Often, that's all they ask in return. Their time is precious and they want to know they're contributing meaningfully. I'm sure you'll be equally glad to do this for someone who asks for your help right?

In seeking help, get [1] the opinions of people who you respect, [2] someone who has the results you want and [3] someone who you feel genuinely cares and can be an objective sounding board. There'll always be perspectives that you miss but others, through their unique experiences and strengths are able to spot. You don't have to take their ideas on board, but keep an open mind and be curious. Very often, all you need is one great idea that becomes a game changer for you.

Apart from your network of friends, another resource we obviously have is Google. More than any other time in history, today, all you need to find ideas, knowledge, tools and systems is available online and often free of charge. Tap into the abundance of online learning, e-books, videos, podcasts of rich, rich information and experience from people who have been there and done that to get more inspiration and ideas. People born one or two generations before you could never dream of having such power and access to the resources that we have today at our fingertips. Through the Internet, you can find a dream job, learn how to brush up your CV, start a home-based business, learn how to trade shares, invest in property, etc. with very little money. Today, through online tools like Fiverr and Upwork, you can literally have a CV written or reviewed professionally for you for five bucks! All it takes is some creativity and the mindset of being willing to give in order to get.

If you need money to pursue a certain course of action and you're short of it, ask, "How can I get it? Who has the money I need? What can I give (skills, time, expertise, other things of value) in return for it?" There will be people in your network who trust you and who have the money — all they need is to know that you're someone they can trust and that you have an abundance mindset — of giving more than you get. Today, you can start a part-time job literally with no money down. You can sell things you no longer want and that others might value through any number of online sites like eBay or Gumtree. All it takes is energy and resourcefulness. Don't have anything to sell? Find someone who does — how about offering to put in all the time and energy and expertise and then going 50-50 on the profits with that person? The options you have today are truly limitless.

Remember, success is never about whether or not you have the resources. It's always about your resourcefulness. Here are a couple of stories that I hope will inspire you.

Starting up an eBay business

Some years ago, one of my friends, Stephanie shared this story with me. She was in her third year of completing an accounting degree at uni and by that time, had realised being an accountant wasn't what she wanted to do for the rest of her life. She had a bright, outgoing personality and found accountancy extremely dull.

She had a boyfriend whose parents were looking to buy a quality treadmill, something Rebel (a popular sports apparel retailer in Australia) was selling for about $2,000. She decided she would scour the Internet to explore her options and came across several online retailers in China who were selling equipment of similar features and functions for about $600. After some careful research, including checking reviews and interviewing previous customers who had dealings with those websites, she decided to order one. Her boyfriend's parents were absolutely delighted with the purchase and were soon raving about it to others. She immediately thought, "Hmm. What's GREAT about this? This could be a business opportunity. Imagine how many other people I could help with this?" So she immediately ordered two more machines, learned to create an ad on eBay and sold them both for $900 each, a cool profit of $600 for not a lot of effort. What did she do next? She ordered four. Sold all four for $900 in quick time and then ordered eight. Six months after she started her business, she had rented a room of a warehouse owned by her boyfriend's parents and was selling an item a day and making a clean profit of $300 per item. On top of that, she had sourced and had begun selling a second item — backyard trampolines. Do the sums. That's about $109K gross salary for the one item for an effort of something like 15 hours a week ($150 per hour), dealing with orders, returns, packaging and shipping.

Prior to the Internet, setting up a business like this would be much riskier and have required significantly more capital. Today, anyone could set up their own home-based business — all it takes is some research to identify a problem that people have, source a product or solution to their problem that they'd pay for and then be resourceful and creative in setting up an online store that works for you 24/7 with minimal overheads.

There's absolutely nothing wrong with being a paid employee today for something that you're passionate about. With the pace of change and disruption today, I truly hope you understand that a myriad of possibilities are easily available that were not before. It doesn't take nearly as much as it once did, to take charge of your own future and decide to be an entrepreneur (and you can make a decent living out of it). All it takes is a dream, a healthy dose of passion, a way to create value for others, and to be remunerated for it (by identifying a problem that people have and offering a solution). Finally, it takes the commitment to make it work and the mindset of always giving more than you receive!

Making our first online sale

About seven years ago, my eldest son Jeremy, who was then in the middle of his Year 12 in high school came to me and said, "Dad, my laptop has broken down. I need a new computer." I had an older model laptop that wasn't used and offered that to him. Problem is – my son didn't just want a computer – he wanted an Apple MacBook Pro – just like the one his dad had. Now, ever since I started my personal transformation journey, I learned that the best gift you can offer others is to help them grow. To find their resourcefulness from within. You've heard the saying "Give a man a fish and you feed him for a day. Teach a man to fish and you feed him for life", right? So Sue and I had agreed many years ago that a philosophy we have for bringing up our kids was to allow them to have anything they wanted in life, as long as it was good for them and that they were willing to earn it. After all, life indeed is like a farm. You gotta sow what you wish to reap.

So I said to my son, "How much will that cost?"

"About two grand", he responded.

"Well, how much have you saved up?" I asked.

"Not much."

He had stopped working part-time to focus on his Year 12 studies (something his parents were glad about). So I said, "OK, what are you willing to do to earn it?"

"Dad, I'm in Year 12. It's a very busy year. I just don't have the time. We had agreed for me to stop working this year. It'll take me ages to make $2,000. It's time I just don't have and can ill-afford to put in right now."

Remember I suggested that whenever you're thinking, "I can't", it's important to start asking, "How can I?" So I said, "OK, let's start by being totally clear and specific about your ideal outcome. Let's come up with a vision statement." Together we came up his vision, which was "To make $2K to purchase a MacBook Pro computer as soon as possible (he was willing to use my old laptop in the interim) with a minimal investment of time."

Then I asked him the "Purpose Why" — "How important is it for you to do this?" Jeremy said, "The other laptop is so old, heavy and clunky, a new laptop would help me to be so much more productive. I have a pretty intensive year with studies and I'm also releasing some new singles with my band and a MacBook Pro would give me some excellent tools for that!'" I nodded and said, "What else is important?" "Well, investing in a good computer that's going to last for quite a few years is going to save us a lot of time and angst in the long run." (I could tell by how animated he was that he was pretty motivated about this.)

So I said, "Great! Let's move on to the next step in the Success Strategy then. What will *you* do? What resources can you tap into to make this happen? Well first, let's look at time. Imagine for now we could achieve this, how much time would you be willing to put into this?" He says, "I guess I'd be willing to put in a full day's effort to get that return. But I really couldn't afford to put in more time than that. But dad, making $2,000 in eight hours – that would be impossible!"

"Well, before we decide if it's impossible or not, given someone else has probably made that happen before, let's brainstorm some options. What *could* we do to make $2,000 with an outlay of eight hours?" Out of the many options we came up with, we really liked this one: I said to him. "I have a resource you may be able to take advantage of. It's an old Mitsubishi Pajero. I've traded it in for a new car that I'm picking up in a couple of months time, but the dealer has only offered me $1K for my trade-in. I think it's worth much more than that, but rather than invest my time and energy to try to make a little more from it, I've decided my time is best spent doing what I love doing best – designing and running more workshops or coaching. So, perhaps you might be willing to do some research, see how much we might get for it via a private sale and if you then decide it's worth your time and effort to put a shine on the car, take pictures, learn to put it up on the Internet and sell it through that medium, any money we make above $1K, we go 50-50 on it. How would you feel about that?"

He excitedly did some research and came back triumphantly – "Dad, there are cars of similar age and condition selling for six to seven grand!"

"I thought that might be the case", I replied. "But remember our ideal goal. We both want it sold quickly — neither you nor I have time for a prolonged sales campaign, entertaining prospective buyers who are not really serious buyers, etc. So why don't you find out what you need to price it at so we can sell it within 24 hours." We decided that if we priced it aggressively at $5K, we should be able achieve our outcome.

I can still picture that bright sunny Sunday. Jeremy outside with his top off and boom box blaring away with him cleaning the car until it was spotless. He took some pictures and crafted up a short ad, which I then gave him some help with.

He did some research on how to post the ad on carsales.com.au and a couple of hours later, our ad was live.

We sold our car to the very first prospective buyer the very next day for $5K. Jeremy and I made $2K more each (for less than eight hours effort and around a $70 fee for the ad). He was able to purchase the computer he wanted and was richer for the new skills he gained on how to trade on the Internet. Much more importantly, he had gained another powerful lesson that whatever he wanted to achieve in life, he could achieve as long as he was prepared to be resourceful enough, was willing to get out of his comfort zone, work hard for it and had the "How can I" mindset. I know this will serve my son well for the rest of his life.

I said to my son, "How many people do you know in this world who, like your dad, have an asset, are time-poor and might be more than delighted to take up on your services and expertise to help them sell their car at a better price than they could get through a trade-in? Imagine being able to make $2,000 or more a day just doing that?"

So life today, my dear friend is full of opportunities just sitting out there, waiting for us to exercise our resourcefulness and creativity. It's never about whether or not you have the resources, but your resourcefulness that matters. It takes a certain way of thinking or a mind-set. It starts with making yourself accountable for whatever you want, being clear about your vision and purpose, and then exercising your resourcefulness in tapping into all the resources you have around you (with the mindset of creating value for others and giving more than you receive). Finally the willingness to have a "whatever it takes" mindset to get out of your comfort zone to make the impossible possible.

If You Can't You Must

Very often, the actions you need to take to get what you want can be pretty daunting and downright scary. That's ok. No, in fact, that's GREAT! If taking that action is good for you and will serve the greater good, make taking that action a must! Remember, nothing changes if nothing changes.

Over the years, I've put together a large collection of great quotes from my favourite philosophers and teachers. Right up there amongst my favourites must be this one by Tony Robbins. He once said to me: "If you're committed to living your most extraordinary life, make this saying not just a mantra, but something you hold dear to you at the deepest level — "If I can't, I must and if I must, I can[8]."

Meaning, whatever your brain tells you "you can't do", if that thing is good for you and will serve the greater good, just do it. This is how you choose to make your spiritual need for growth a priority over the ego's need for certainty or comfort. Learning to be comfortable while being vulnerable is one of the greatest skills you can develop. Master this and the possibilities are endless.

Holding this philosophy close to my heart has made such a great difference to my life. When I learned this, I decided to put this into practise immediately. When I asked myself, *"If today was my last day at my workplace, what would I do to make the biggest, most positive and meaningful difference to my colleagues and family around me and in a way that will move me towards my vision?",* the following came up: "Teach your team what you've learned."

My heart raced with anxiety at that suggestion and my brain responded with, "You're not qualified. They'll laugh at you. You're not a speaker, or trainer. You're a nerdy geek. You don't have the right qualifications. You don't have any materials. You won't have time to practise. Your colleagues will probably say they're too busy." This went on and on, further creating doubt and uncertainty.

I was prepared for this response though. After all, I knew my brain was just doing its best to protect me. And having learned that being comfortable and protected didn't equate to being fulfilled, I said to my brain, "Thank you for that loving feedback! Not now!" In taking action that's out of your comfort zone, do whatever it takes to set yourself up for success.

Some are ready to take a bold and dramatic step forward. Some are more comfortable taking that first small step forward. My sons, Jeremy and Aaron are much more of the former. Throughout their youth, apart from Aaron's love for hip-hop dance, both boys were never big on sport. They'd always participated (giving soccer, tennis, swimming and even cricket a go at school) and always given their best, but it was never their cup of tea. They were definitely far more creative (excelling in the arts and communication), and had great people skills.

Just under three years ago, both decided they wanted to get "jacked" and got into powerlifting. When these guys decide on something, there's no half-measures about it. They started working out six days a week, hired a coach so they'd do it the right way and quickly. They radically changed their diet (causing great angst to their mum, who loved cooking for her children and found it difficult to keep up with their ever-changing routine) and started devoting much of their spare time viewing YouTube videos on how to get fit, create an amazing physique, and most importantly, develop their strength. Within six months, they'd set their sights on their first powerlifting competition and just six months ago, competed at their first Nationals.

For others, starting first with baby steps works best. If such people were to set a huge goal, it'd often result in procrastination, which can only lead to even greater self-doubt. In taking those first steps forward, the initial goal is to create certainty and self-belief that "you can", not about the result you produce.

I remember reading an article where a clinical psychologist attended to a client who was a middle-aged single mother, highly stressed, had several mouths to feed, and a busy day job. Every evening, after cooking and cleaning up, she simply did not feel like she had any energy for anything else but to zonk out in front of her telly. She was overweight and depressed. The psychologist said that upon first meeting her, the logical recommendation was obvious - to get her into a personal fitness program and to lose some weight. This would help her create more energy, improve her self-esteem and start the positive cycle of creating a better future.

However, his experience told him that if he were to suggest this to her, he would never see her again. The lady was simply feeling too overwhelmed to feel like she could muster the time and investment required for a gym membership and coach. So he suggested to her a simple game-plan. He said, "All I want you to do is when you're watching the telly this week, instead of sitting down the whole time, just stand up and walk on the spot for 10 minutes. Can you handle that?" She said, "yes, sure, I can do that." A week later, she came back, chuffed at being able to report she'd succeeded in following through on her commitment. He was then able to set the bar higher to 15 minutes. He continued building on the success and self-esteem of getting her to take small steps out of her comfort zone regularly. The confidence-building phase led her to taking on much bigger challenges, which eventually had a massive, positive effect on the direction for her life.

So know yourself. If you're like my sons and into massive and radical transformation, go for it. If you're not and work better with baby steps, that's ok. The main thing is this: DO SOMETHING! Make PROGRESS!

For me, my baby step towards teaching my staff what I'd learned was to first invite just a few people from my close network of friends at work to the very first workshop I'd ever run, on the topic of resilience and emotional intelligence. I drafted an email that said, "You've commented on how you've seen me change and grow over the past few months. If you're seriously interested in learning what I've learned, then next Tuesday, bring along a brown bag for lunch and I'll run a brief presentation on how to effectively set goals." It took me seconds to draft that email, but hours before I could summon up the courage to press the Send button. Self-doubt kept creeping in and the voices in my head did its best to sabotage my aspirations.

Eventually, I told myself that all my life, I'd been living by the "Ready. Aim. Fire" paradigm of success. In truth, it was more like "Ready. Aim. Aim ... Aim ... Ready ... Aim ..." Procrastination was a regular friend. It was "paralysis through analysis". People I really admired and whose life I wanted to be more like — the Richard Bransons, Steve Irwins of this world, lived by the paradigm "Ready! Fire! Aim!" Their philosophy, which had started to really make sense to me was "if it doesn't work the first time, just learn from it and take the next step". "There is no failure, only feedback".

I also reminded myself "insanity was in fact doing the same things over and over again and expecting a different result". That "if I can't, I must! And if I must, I can!" And so, I just pressed "Send". My stress levels instantly shot through the roof and I heard myself saying, "I hope no one replies. I hope it ends up in their Junk Folder. What if I don't get my materials in on time?"

But the next day, as soon as I saw a number of "Accepts" arrive at my inbox, I knew I was committed. A week later, magically it seemed, my PowerPoint presentation was ready. I was nervous. My fear of rejection was debilitating. To manage my emotions, I kept reminding myself of the belief that if I faced rejection, it wouldn't be them rejecting me personally, but my ideas or the quality of the presentation. I reminded myself that I was giving them a gift and if they turned it down, it wasn't my problem. And I applied all the strategies I'd learned about getting into a peak state of confidence, passion and contribution. As part of the preparation for that presentation, I arrived early and warmed up by moving the way I wanted to feel — positive and confident. I repeated the following affirmations again and again to myself, "I am courage! I am faith! I am love! And I am fun!" And within seconds, I felt ready.

I gave that presentation my all that day. I was grateful and encouraged by the body language of my audience who sat there, seemingly spellbound or simply shocked at this side of me they'd seldom witnessed — all passion and enthusiasm.

By the end of that presentation, they said they wanted more, that this training was certainly more valuable than all the technical training they'd attended on DB2 and WebSphere. They asked if we could make this a monthly ritual. I was so encouraged I said "Why not?" That monthly experience started to grow and soon, I had some of them asking me if we could extend our reach and invite colleagues from other departments. My confidence grew and the energy and positivity I had from that helped me grow.

My journey to being an inspirational speaker and transformation coach started the second I decided to press that Send button. It was driven not by any intention of seeking a different career but inspired by the thought, "If this were my last day, what would I do today to make the biggest difference to others around me?" By consciously choosing to make meeting my higher order needs of contribution and growth a priority (over certainty), my journey started to take a different tangent. I shall forever be grateful for that decision. Each workshop I ran drew a slightly larger audience and soon, my manager had heard about my work and invited me to run a team building session for the Sales organisation. My positive energy and contributions were allowing me to exert positive influence on key decision makers I never before felt possible. When I focussed on changing others, my influence of others shrank. When I focussed purely on transforming me, I started to draw others into my sphere of influence.

So understand this – the best way to influence others is to first seek to change the only person you have total control over. Yourself.

So what would you do today to make the biggest difference to your organisation, others around you, and stretch yourself out of your comfort zone? Just take that action, my friend, and life will magically start working even more for you!

Action Plan

1. Review the Vision and Purpose you set.

2. Ask yourself, "If this were the last week I was at my work, what would I do to make the biggest difference to my organisation?" Write these goals down.

3. Reflect on "What resources can I tap into, both external and internal, that will help me advance these goals?"

4. Decide when you'll accomplish this goal, how much time you'll allocate to it, and how it will help you feel to follow through on a commitment you've made to yourself.

CHAPTER 9

Epilogue – Putting it all together

Thirty years ago, my younger brother Gregory came to study in Sydney. We'd always been close and we shared the same apartment. He struggled with his HSC that year and despite always being a decent student, his grades were significantly below his expectations. He managed to get into Newcastle University but after the first six months, it was clear he was struggling to cope. He was just scraping through a couple of subjects and not getting through the rest, quite unlike what we felt he was capable of. He wrote me a rambling note one day, complaining about headaches and hallucinations and finding it difficult to concentrate, and confided in me of his fears as someone had suggested that he see a psychiatrist.

I can only imagine how worried he must have been in. Back then in Malaysia where we grew up, it wasn't common for someone to consult a psychologist, let alone a psychiatrist. This was for people who were going to be sent to "mental wards". The words alone would conjure up images of a place where people were put into a straightjacket, locked up and the "keys thrown away". Greg (or Gary as he's always been lovingly called at home) was diagnosed with schizophrenia, a condition we barely understood at the time.

Thanks to the help of our dear friend Father Paul Stenhouse (a wonderful chaplain to many overseas students who studied in Sydney), we managed to have Gary transferred back to a uni in Sydney so he could live under the care of my brothers and I. Not having seen Gary for about eight months (since he moved to Newcastle), the change in his behaviour was stark. A once cheery, friendly, soft-spoken, warm man had become moody, suspicious, erratic, angry, verbally abusive at times and often irrational in his thought and actions. He'd lock himself up in his room for hours, often emerging just to have a meal and at times, would consume everything that was laid out in front of him without consideration of others who hadn't eaten. He continued to struggle with his studies, often laying the blame on me for not devoting the time to help him with his assignments.

The struggle continued for another 18 months or so. In February 1989, my bride and I decided to marry and, with my siblings, returned home to Malaysia to celebrate this occasion with our families. It was the first time Gary had been home after being in Australia for about three years. My parents and I and my two other brothers – Chris and Ben — discussed Gary's situation and with an incredibly heavy heart, decided to pull the plug on his studies. The pressure and accompanying stress of completing university (which he had become obsessed with) was doing his condition more harm than good, let alone the tremendous financial drain it had been on my parents. Looking back now, I realise how challenging that decision must have been particularly on my parents and Gary.

For my parents, they would have considered the real possibility that in their retirement years, they might have to spend the rest of their lives looking after someone they dearly loved who was possibly incapable of making a living, and dealing with a condition they knew so little about. Since we've learned about schizophrenia, we now understand it so much better. But ignorance breeds fear, and back then in Malaysia it would have been taboo to talk about someone in the family with a condition like Gary. It was considered a "reflection of poor upbringing". So it was particularly difficult for my parents as there weren't many people they felt they could turn to for understanding and help. I can't start to imagine the mental, spiritual and emotional impact that decision would have had on Gary. He didn't take it well at all and I must say that moment when we broke the news to him and his reaction to it, to this day, was the saddest day of my life. I felt like I had let him and my parents down.

While my brothers and I struggled to deal with this, I must admit on the other hand to secretly being relieved that Gary wasn't in our face every day. My coping strategy was to sweep it under the rug and hope and pray that somehow, intervention from above would make things better. My reasoning was that "if the experts say there isn't a cure, what could I, a computer programmer do?"

For a long time, Gary's situation wasn't getting better. It took years for us to convince dad that Gary needed medication – my dad's generation had a pretty myopic view about "drugs" and dad's counsel by wise friends was that Gary would pretty much need to be on medication for the rest of his life. For my dad, no one was going to convince him to turn his son into a "drug addict". Without the assistance of medication, Gary was highly erratic and irrational with his behaviour. In hindsight now, while we were most concerned about how my parents would cope, I can only imagine how much this fear would have been magnified for Gary. His ability to remain "sane" all those years, while hearing voices he couldn't control, and the lack of certainty about his future, while the people he cared about most constantly reprimanded him for his behaviour, always reminds me of how incredibly resilient we humans really are and the capacity we have for love and forgiveness. Gary exemplifies all of these attributes.

The problem with a condition like schizophrenia (which at its root is caused by a chemical imbalance in the brain) is that to others, the symptoms are behavioural, not physical (not visibly at least). And our social conditioning informs us that when someone isn't behaving in a way we expect, our remedy is that we need to correct such behaviour. Reprimands, scolding, "Why are you like that?" (of the blame variety) would have been common for Gary, and his behaviour during that time (eating too much, sleeping too much, hiding away in his room, and acting rebellious) would have been his subconscious attempts to have a measure of control over a situation that he just had no control over.

My parents would have felt so lonely during that period. All of us were affected, particularly my dad. Well-meaning friends and relatives and even his sons were often harsh with Gary (due to their protective instincts for my parents), which made matters worse. Gary's reactions were harshest to those he felt most safe with, and my parents would have taken the brunt of his tantrums during those difficult periods.

Somehow, dad's intuition told him that a disciplinary approach wasn't the answer. Deep down, he instinctively understood that what Gary most needed was empathy, understanding and compassion. He needed someone he could trust, talk to, pour out his fears to and who could finally guide him, with baby steps, to move forward constructively. He certainly could do with a huge dose of optimism, the faith that everything happens for a reason, and it's going to turn out ok. Turns out, all of us could have done with healthy doses of that too at the time.

It was challenging both spiritually and financially for my parents. The medical system for such conditions in Malaysia was quite ineffective at the time and it was suggested that Gary seek treatment in Singapore. I can only imagine the days when dad and Gary would take the eight-hour train ride from Seremban to Singapore, for a 15-minute appointment where a specialist (typically coming across as cold and uncaring and looking like someone who could do with the medication himself), asked a few questions, didn't seem to have any answers, prescribed some medication and a whopping bill (which would have been about half my dad's monthly pension at the time).

For years, all of us felt fearful, worried and helpless about Gary's situation. Guess what question we were asking again and again and again? Yes, the "Blame Why". The answers were debilitating: "We should have spent more time with him when he was younger. We're paying for our sins. We shouldn't have put so much pressure on him". They were neither assuring nor constructive.

I remember the day I reflected on the following question: "If a doctor came to me and said that I only had six months left, what would I do with the rest of my time?" The answers were "teach my children everything I can about emotional intelligence, resilience and fulfilment. Then when I left this world, I would have taught them how to fish, rather than giving them fish, and they'd be ok."

Secondly, I thought about my parents. Their biggest worry was about who would look after Gary when they were gone. Their eldest two sons had migrated to Australia and the youngest was in the process, and while we assured them that everything would be ok, I also know the saying "talk is cheap". My greatest fear at the time was of getting that late-night phone call, knowing that one of them could possibly be departing with worry, when they deserved only to feel like they had been the most successful parents we could ever hope to have.

And so, I decided with new resolve that if I were given only six months to live, I would find a way to help my brother find his feet and confidence again and in the process, give my parents the reassurance that all would be ok. I wanted my actions to do the talking and by that time was convinced that everything that had happened (my challenging period at IBM followed by starting to enjoy my job more than ever when I started running my Tuesday brown bag lunch sessions) was simply the universe's way of waking me up to find my true calling in life — to pass the invaluable skills I'd learned to others around me, particularly my family. Not long after I made this decision, I received that fateful phone call about my dad's impending surgery.

The two weeks I spent with dad by his hospital bed gave me the quality time I needed both for myself and also to be able to share what I'd learned with dad. Without fail, Gary would show up every day to be by my dad's side. He wouldn't say a word, just stand there for a few minutes but always had a little gift for my dad — it might have been a pad of writing paper or just a bottle of drinking water. Ever since he'd been on meds, his condition had stabilised to the extent that my dad had been able to convince him to help him with some badminton coaching and through that, he was able to make some money. Not much, but it was enough that it would have been meaningful for him. He's one of the most generous souls I know.

I taught my dad all the things I'd learned, about being resilient, about the power of the mind, about simply choosing to be optimistic and finding fulfilment no matter what. When I asked my dad how he had become so ill so suddenly, he confided in me that it was as much psychological as it was physical. He had just retired from being an international badminton referee and for years had dreaded the big retirement day. He confided in me that when he retired, he felt like his life had ended. While he had been a tremendous carer for Gary for so many years, his service to a sport he loved was an important outlet for his need for growth and contribution. He confided to me that when he retired, it felt like a huge void had come into his life that could not be filled. He felt a deep sense of guilt about having to stay home for the rest of his life, facing a son whose condition he felt particularly helpless about.

I told him about the power of reflecting on "what's great about this?" On reflecting about this, he said there was so much to be grateful about Gary's situation:

- Unlike many who resort to illicit drugs and alcohol to distract them from fear and uncertainty and refused to get on medication, we had been successful in convincing Gary to be on medication. And while the side effects of the medication often made him drowsy and listless, he was often more rational when he was on it.

- He looked after his grooming well, dressed well and went to church regularly. Mass and prayer and having

- Another "heavenly family" he could always count on seemed to give Gary a deep sense of peace and centred him.

- My dad said that Gary's situation had deepened the bonds within our family members, and he and mum felt supported.

- We had a kind Samaritan neighbour and several wonderful friends who had earned Gary's trust and who Gary would regularly visit for counselling.

- Gary had also found a counsellor at the local hospital that he had connected with and could count on for support and advice.

- My dad said that learning about schizophrenia had also helped him develop a deeper empathy for others. That he now realised Gary's condition was much more prevalent than he had imagined and that he used to judge others who had a family member with a mental illness, but could now show them greater compassion.

- I shared with dad that I was grateful that at that time, Gary could be at dad's side, without having to deal with the stress of having to take a leave of absence from work. That Gary, in spite of everything he'd been through, was probably the kindest, most generous soul I knew – he never forgot any of our birthdays and would take the trouble to write us cards and send us gifts.

Just reflecting on this together made us feel grateful and more empowered about the situation we were in.

I then asked my dad the next question, "If anything were possible, where do you see yourself five years from now? What would the ideal situation be?"

My dad thought about it and said, "There's not much more I can do to help with my son's recovery, I don't think I'm qualified, but I've realised that the people who often need the most help are carers. I've seen parents fight with each other and lose their relationships in the process, blaming each other for their child's predicament purely out of a feeling of helplessness and ignorance about the condition. There's so much I can do to help them." My dad resolved to set up the first mental health association in my hometown of Seremban, to create an avenue where carers could come for help, advice, or just feel like there was someone else they could share their worries with.

Another date I will always cherish is 10 October 2010. This was the day Malaysia held its first-ever Mental Health Awareness week. In my hometown of Seremban, my dad helped coordinate an event to commemorate this occasion and a talk for about 60 carers. I was proud to be invited to deliver a presentation that day to these 60 wonderful people, about the power of emotional intelligence and resilience.

That day, I felt incredibly blessed to invite my brother Gary to say a few words. He spent just a few minutes giving the audience a ray of hope, sharing his personal story of transformation and the road to recovery. How through his faith, the unconditional love of his parents and the help of good friends, he had been through the worst and was now able to cope and live a productive life where he was more comfortable socialising with others.

Today, Gary is better than he's ever been. He's the same loving, tender, kind, generous soul who provides comfort to my parents through his presence. He lives a productive life and continues to coach badminton with my dad, who turned 80 last year. He's appreciated by friends he regularly socialises with, contributes to the church in his own way (occasionally singing in the church choir) and can stride forward with greater strength and hope than ever. Every now and then, whenever he feels an onset of anxiety attacks, he takes a power walk outside and "moves how he wants to feel". After striding with strength and confidence and repeating the affirmations "I am courage! I am strength! I am a leader! I can achieve anything I set my mind to" for five to 10 minutes, he says the anxiety dissipates and he feels in control again.

Mum and dad, who are 78 and 80 respectively, are as strong, happy and healthy as we could have hoped, for a couple of their vintage. They lead a quiet, simple and productive life, much loved by good friends and ever willing to help make the lives of others better, mine included. They are my ultimate models of resilience. What's the ultimate secret of their success? Loving and giving even when that's what they feel least like doing and being there to support the other.

Every time we meet or talk over the phone, Gary thanks me for the tapes I've given him empowering him to cope with the condition, the vitamin supplements I've provided which help negate some of the side effects of his medication, and the coaching I've given him. My sincere response to him always is that he is the one who's saved me, who's given me the courage and strength to live a most extraordinarily fulfilling life. I remind him that his situation and the decisions my parents made have contributed to my parents today having tremendous vitality and leading a purposeful life filled with grace and gratitude. My brother's condition and my desire to be there for my parents was one of the primary motivators for me leaving IBM in 2006, at the peak of my powers (and by that time enjoying what I did at IBM more than I ever did) to set up my own coaching and training consultancy on transformation, leadership, resilience and emotional intelligence.

I hope you can understand why I'm so passionate about sharing all of this with you in this book. Imagine if indeed your brain was programed and conditioned with an operating system that would respond like this in every situation:

"What's great about this?" – filling you with gratitude

"What do I really want? – lifting you with inspiration

"How is achieving that important?" – injecting a sense of urgency and drive

"What will I do?" – helping you exercise courage

How would your life be? How resilient would you be? How empowered might you feel in times of disruptive change?

In life, there are truly lots of things you have no control over. Your environment can affect the way you feel, but you have the power to choose your response. Decide each and every day to make it the most outstanding day you deserve — life indeed is way too short — for yourself and those around you. Create and choose to be in the most beautiful states you deserve and put that into what you do. When in doubt, always choose love over fear. Know that you and you alone have total power over how you move, think, speak, feel and act and this enables you to be the master of your destiny.

All the resources you need to experience every success and happiness in the world you deserve are already within you. Make your life the masterpiece it was always designed to be! I am humbled and thank you for allowing me to share a little in your journey.

ACKNOWLEDGEMENTS

This book has been six years in the making. The process has often been arduous. Writing is not easy for me and not particularly fun when you're working with deadlines, even if they're self-imposed. I'll eternally be grateful to Stacey Kuyf, my editor and writing coach, Nadine Fischer, who did such a thorough job proof-reading the manuscript and Nyrie Roos, who guided me through the entire process - not just for making this book so much easier and more pleasant to read but for their coaching, encouragement, flexibility and patience. To Julia Kuris, who did such a sensational job with the design of this book cover - thank you for your creativity and for being such a pleasure to work with.

To my children Jem, Aaron, and Courtney. Know that you are my primary inspiration for this book. Whenever things got tough, just reconnecting with the reason I started this journey – to put in writing some of the principles and philosophies that have helped me lead such a fulfilling life so that you (and some day your children, should you decide to have them) may benefit – has never failed to get me out of the trough.

Jem, thanks for being my chief critic — giving me not just the straight talk I needed about working harder to make it something I am truly proud of but also the benefit of your composition experience and the reassuring encouragement that you felt this was worthwhile and something you'd not hesitate to encourage your friends to read. Your views have been instrumental in helping me with the final title of this book and the cover design, something that I agonised over for weeks. And yes, I feel truly proud at this final stage of editing of what I've put together.

Aaron, thanks for being such a great sounding board and for your permission to use stories about you in this book. I know it makes you cringe and you probably still wish I didn't, but I'll forever be grateful for your willingness to endure whatever it is you have to endure so others may benefit. I will also always treasure the chat we had which helped me decide that one of my goals for this book would be making it an Amazon best seller. If by chance the book's status persuaded a reader to pick up this book, know that you would have contributed to that reader's future in a meaningful way.

My beautiful Courtney, my shining light — thanks for being so supportive and for your trust and understanding when I've not been around as much as I would've liked to. Know that I couldn't be prouder of you.

Being dad to the three of you is my life's greatest privilege and blessing. I can't wait to read *your* books one day.

To my parents, Francis and Rose, my siblings Chris, Gary and Ben, and Clare — I am who I am largely through your love, sacrifices and through each of you being models of extraordinary resilience and grace. Thank you for being the inspiration you are.

To Tony Robbins, who amongst many other things taught me the true meaning of integrity and many of the principles and strategies of emotional mastery and resilience — your work helped me define the legacy I wanted to create and the courage and tools to break through to the future I have today, one filled with infinite possibilities.

And to my extraordinary "Robbins" family of trainers and leaders — thanks for walking with me in my journey and helping transform the shy, nerdy geek to one who's not afraid to love and live life to the fullest. A special thanks to my NLP Coach, Steve Linder, for instilling in me the virtue of "transforming from the heart" and Rajeev Dewan for the generous sharing of your writing experience. It helped me understand what I was to go through and gave me the timely boost I needed to get this off the ground.

To the many wonderful people who've attended my coaching, workshops and training — know that working with you has taught me much and given me some of the most fulfilling experiences of my career, not to mention enabling me to see so much of the beautiful world we live in. Many of you have asked if I had or could write a book. Thank you for your faith and for believing in me. This book is written also for you and yours.

To my partners in crime — Adel Khreich, Michael Chachaty, the exceptional team at Blue Visions Management, the Institute of Management, Steven Loo, Marcus Heng and Ratna Juita at Stevenson Hureca — thanks for your trust, for being so much fun to work with, for sharing our passion of making a difference through what we do and for your help in opening the many doors that have enabled our work to traverse 10 countries and more than 100 organisations.

To my best friend Julian, now the Archbishop of Kuala Lumpur, Malaysia. Know that your silent wisdom helped me through the most challenging periods of my life. I couldn't be prouder of you or feel more blessed for your friendship and prayers all these years.

To my former colleagues at grapeVINE Technologies and IBM Australia — thank you for being such a precious part of the formative years of my career. Know that the experience I gained, working with some of the most intelligent, passionate, professional and competent people I have been blessed to come across, is being put to good use to benefit other leaders and aspiring leaders. I owe a massive debt of gratitude to the late Professor Cyril Brookes for giving me the best start to my career I could have wished for, which led me to settle down in the most beautiful place on earth – Sydney, Australia. A special thank you to Angela Mihalarias, Karen Taylor, Mike Deggs and Sunny Wan, who graciously attended the first workshop I ever ran during my time at IBM and Michael Graf, my former manager whose encouragement to fulfil that nagging inner voice was reassuring when I was feeling the most vulnerable.

My Usana experience taught me the essence of true health and true wealth and gave me a platform to give a voice to what I truly believed in. To my mentors, in particular Virend Singh, Eddie Kim, Raphael Ahn and the many associates I have had the blessing to learn and work with, thank you for your guidance, inspiration and trust.

To Bernard Lee, my quality assurance manager for much of the work I do - thank you for your incredible patience and ever being willing to take on the myriad of detail that enables us to go the extra mile with everything we do – I am so glad I have you at my side. Thank you for putting up with my seemingly endless stream of last minute SOS-es.

To my extended family, classmates and friends who have been cheering me from the sidelines throughout this writing journey - your encouragement and support has meant the world to me. An especially heartfelt thank you to Lay Ean Eng, for introducing me to Pam Brossman and her 30-day Book challenge. To my niece Rosanne Lo who helped me fine-tune my manuscript and who helped shape three key characters in this plot — Blame Why, Curious Why and Purpose Why. You'd make a fantastic professional editor.

To my dearest dear, Sue. Know that my journey would neither be possible, complete nor worthwhile without you by my side. Thank you for being my greatest champion, for believing in me and for your unconditional love and support. That moment you said, "do what you're meant to do" with confidence and love gave me the lift and belief to take the leap of faith. Know that your smile lights up my day and makes me believe I can achieve and be anything I choose to be.

And finally to my heavenly Father, whose loving hands guide my every step and through whom I know that all is possible – thank you for the majesty of your every creation. I am humbled for the extraordinary blessings you continue to shower on my family and on me each and every day.

About the Author
Dominic Siow

Dominic Siow is transformation coach, keynote speaker and trainer. A reformed introverted "nerdy geek", he found his life's true calling in 2006. Leaving the security of a senior management position at IBM Australia, he and his wife Sue founded EQ Strategist, a consultancy with a mission to create empowering, high performance workplace culture where people are inspired to bring their "A" game to work each and every day. Since then, his training, coaching and talks have touched the lives of more than 20,000 people in over 100 blue chip and public sector organisations across the Asia-Pacific and Middle East regions.He is an expert in human potential development, transformational leadership, change management, emotional intelligence, project leadership, resilience and influence. A man who sees and brings out the best in people, his courses are frequently rated by participants as the "best professional and personal development they've ever encountered". Prior to his present vocation, Dominic was VP of Product Development for an Australian knowledge management start-up called grapeVINE Technologies during which he had the privilege of building high performance project teams both in Australia and the Silicon Valley, USA. He also ran a consulting practice for IBM Software Group and was Head of Operations for its Software Services division.

During times when disruption and change is an everyday occurrence in the workplace, fear, uncertainty and self-doubt can cripple our decision-making, productivity and zest for work and life. "What's GREAT about this? How to be Resilient and Thrive through Disruption and Change" is a practical and inspiring read that will give the skills and techniques to think, feel, act and be in your best and most resourceful state in order to find and capitalise on the opportunities that present themselves in every situation.

This book taps into the wisdom of the ages, contemporary research in neuroscience, and the author's personal application of these principles to turn around an I.T. career that had gone pear-shaped after losing 30% of his team to an organisational restructure. For two years, he went through a period of debilitating self-doubt, anxiety and stress, which affected him both professionally and personally.

Learning about emotional intelligence and the power of a positive mind-set has turned his life around. This book includes action plans and reflections and draws on his personal journey of transformation from an introverted, shy geek to an international inspirational speaker, coach and trainer who has and continues to impact thousands of lives across the globe.

Connect with Dominic!

*Scan this QR code with your smart phone
to visit our website:*
http://www.eqstrategist.com/home.html

And visit us on Facebook, Twitter and Linkedin

https://www.facebook.com/emotionalintelligencetraining

https://twitter.com/dominicsiow

https://www.linkedin.com/in/dominicsiow/

References

Prelude

[1] **New York bestselling author Simon Sinek**: Shandrow, K. (2014). *The 5 Most Popular TED talks of all time.* [online] Entrepreneur. Available at: https://www.entrepreneur.com/article/239672 [Accessed 4th Mar. 2017].

Chapter 1: Let's Get Started

[1] **a YouTube video that showed a man and a woman, a few steps apart, riding up an escalator**:

MotivatingSuccess (2012). *Stuck on an Escalator: Take Action.* [video]. Available at: https://www.youtube.com/watch?v=VrSUe_m19FY [Accessed 6th Mar. 2017].

[2] **Amongst his many business ventures, Branson**: bio, (2015). Richard Branson Biography. [online] Available at:

http://www.biography.com/people/richard-branson-9224520 [Accessed 6th Mar. 2017].

[3] **Tony Fernandes, the wonderful entrepreneur who founded Air Asia:**

Topham, G. (2014). AirAsia tycoon followed in Richard Branson's footsteps. [online] The Irish Times. Available at:

http://www.irishtimes.com/news/world/asia-pacific/airasia-tycoon-followed-in-richard-branson-s-footsteps-1.2049869 [Accessed 5th Mar. 2017].

[4] **Branson wrote in his autobiography of the decision to start an airline**:

Telegraph.co.uk. *Sir Richard Branson and the birth of Virgin*. [online] Available at: http://www.telegraph.co.uk/finance/financetopics/profiles/6965490/Sir-Richard-Branson-and-the-birth-of-Virgin.html [Accessed 5th Mar. 2017].

[5] **In her tribute to her husband, "My Steve"**: Irwin, T. (2007). *My Steve.*: Simon & Schuster.

Chapter 2: Disruption and Change – the New Norm

[1] **YouTube video presentation titled "***Did you know? - Shift Happens***"**:

EvolvMyLife. (2008). *Did You Know 3.0 - Shift Happens (Official Video HD)*. [video]. Available at: https://www.youtube.com/watch?v=F9WDtQ4Ujn8 [Accessed 5th Mar. 2017].

[2] **Harvard Business School professor and disruption guru .... Clayton Christensen:**

Howard, C. (2013). *Disruption Vs. Innovation: What's The Difference?* [online] Forbes. Available at: https://www.forbes.com/sites/carolinehoward/2013/03/27/you-say-innovator-i-say-disruptor-whats-the-difference/#70d55f1d6f43 [Accessed 5th Mar. 2017].

[3] **In 2013, "Inocente" became the first Kickstarter-funded film .....**

Watercutter, A. (2013). *The First Kickstarter Film to Win an Oscar Takes Home Crowdsourced Gold.* [online] Wired. Available at: https://www.wired.com/2013/02/kickstarter-first-oscar/?+wired%252Findex+(Wired%253A+Top+Stories [Accessed 5th Mar. 2017].

⁴ **In cities from Kuala Lumpur to Jakarta to Paris ….**

Zulaika, I. (2016). The Current Uber versus Taxi Turf War: Looking for a Win-Win Solution. [online] malaysiandigest.com

Available at: http://malaysiandigest.com/frontpage/282-maintile/608162-the-current-uber-vs-taxi-turf-war-looking-for-a-win-win-solution.html [Accessed 5th Mar. 2017].

⁵ **By the first quarter of 2016, Didi Chuxing had 85% ….**

Makinen, J. (2016). *In Didi Chuxing, Uber finally met its match.* [online] Los Angeles Times. Available at: http://www.latimes.com/world/asia/la-fi-uber-china-didi-sale-20160801-snap-story.html [Accessed 5th Mar. 2017].

⁵ **Travis Kalanick, famously said the company had been losing $1 billion ….**

Makinen, J. (2016). *In Didi Chuxing, Uber finally met its match.* [online] Los Angeles Times. Available at: http://www.latimes.com/world/asia/la-fi-uber-china-didi-sale-20160801-snap-story.html [Accessed 5th Mar. 2017].

⁵ **In the first quarter of 2015, when Uber was relatively new to China ….**

Makinen, J. (2016). *In Didi Chuxing, Uber finally met its match.* [online] Los Angeles Times. Available at: http://www.latimes.com/world/asia/la-fi-uber-china-didi-sale-20160801-snap-story.html [Accessed 5th Mar. 2017].

⁶ **In 2012, Wechat's extraordinary success as a social media platform …..**

Subrahmanyam, V. (2015). Mobile Technology in China: A Transformation of the Payments Industry. [online] China Research Center. Available at:

http://www.chinacenter.net/2015/china_currents/14-1/mobile-technology-in-china-a-transformation-of-the-payments-industry/

[7] **In China, Uber the disrupter became the disrupted …..**

Mozur, P. and Michael, J. (2016). Uber Rival's $28 Billion Valuation Shows Size of China's Ride-Sharing Market. [online] The New York Times. Available at:

https://www.nytimes.com/2016/06/17/business/international/china-didi-chuxing.html?_r=0 [Accessed 5th Mar. 2017].

[8] **Mine closures have caused the loss of thousands of jobs …..**

Yeomans, J. (2016). *Australia's mining boom turns to dust as commodity prices collapse.* [online] The Telegraph. Available at: http://www.telegraph.co.uk/finance/newsbysector/industry/mining/12142813/Australias-mining-boom-turns-to-dust-as-commodity-prices-collapse.html [Accessed 5th Mar. 2017].

[9] **On 30th April, 2016, the Straits Times of Singapore …..**

Suk-Wai, C. (2016). *The Thai Canal that may change Singapore forever.* [online] The Straits times. Available at: http://www.straitstimes.com/lifestyle/arts/the-thai-canal-that-may-change-singapore-forever [Accessed 5th Mar. 2017].

[10] **Before oil was discovered in the 1950s the UAE's ……**

BBC News, (2016). *United Arab Emirates country profile.* [online] Available at: http://www.bbc.com/news/world-middle-east-14703998 [Accessed 5th Mar. 2017].

[11] **On 8th September, 2016, Reuters reported ….**

French, D., Arnold, T. and Paul, K. (2016). *Exclusive: Saudi Oger faces huge debt restructuring as rescue talks collapse.* Reuters. Available at: http://www.reuters.com/article/us-saudi-oger-restructuring-idUSKCN11E153 [Accessed 5th Mar. 2017].

[12] **By 2020, driverless cars will be pretty standard fare ….**

Adams, T. (2015). *Self-driving cars: from 2020 you will become a permanent backseat driver.* The Guardian. Available at: https://www.theguardian.com/technology/2015/sep/13/self-driving-cars-bmw-google-2020-driving [accessed 6th Mar. 2017].

[13] **As a nation whose economy revolves around a $200 billion …..**

Reynolds, E. (2016). *The jobs killer is coming: How driverless trucks could change Australia.* news.com.au. Available at: http://www.news.com.au/finance/business/travel/the-jobs-killer-is-coming-how-driverless-trucks-could-change-australia/news-story/4f5b8a42b-0452703d62e00f3e7644d7b [Accessed 6thMar. 2017].

[13] **After a futuristic fleet of self-driving "smart trucks" …**

Reynolds, E. (2016). *The jobs killer is coming: How driverless trucks could change Australia.* news.com.au. Available at: http://www.news.com.au/finance/business/travel/the-jobs-killer-is-coming-how-driverless-trucks-could-change-australia/news-story/4f5b8a42b-0452703d62e00f3e7644d7b [Accessed 6thMar. 2017].

[14] **Heed the words of Jim Rohn, one …**

Marr, C. (2015). *The best of Jim Rohn – Chris Marr's top 20 Jim Rohn Quotes.* [Blog] C/M. Available at: http://www.chrismarr.co.uk/the-best-of-jim-rohn/ [Accessed 6th Mar. 2017].

[15] **In Dan Pink's book, *Drive: The Surprising Truth of What Motivates Us*…**

Pink, D. (2009). *Drive: The Surprising Truth About What Motivates Us.* New York: Penguin Group.

[16] **Today, the US labour department predicts …**

Student Career Exploration and Planning Blog, (2010). *What's the Big Deal About Job Hopping and Why Should it Matter to High*

School Students? [blog] Available at: https://studentcareercoach.net/2010/10/13/whats-the-big-deal-about-job-hopping-and-why-should-it-matter-to-high-school-students/ [Accessed 6th Mar. 2017].

[17] I have more power in my phone and smartwatch ...

Puiu, T. (2015). *Your smartphone is millions of times more powerful than all of NASA's combined computing in 1969.* ZME Science. Available at: http://www.zmescience.com/research/technology/smartphone-power-compared-to-apollo-432/ [Accessed 6th Mar 2017].

[18] Al Gore, who first so powerfully ...

Gore, A.(2013). *The Future: Six Drivers of Global Change.* New York: Random House.

[19] He also writes "There ...

Gore, A.(2013). *The Future: Six Drivers of Global Change.* New York: Random House.

Chapter 3: How your EQ affects your Resilience

[1] Let's take a look at some of the biggest layoffs in American history ...

Kline, D. B.(2015). *The biggest layoffs in American History.* The Motley Fool. Available at: https://www.fool.com/investing/general/2015/09/06/the-biggest-layoffs-in-american-history.aspx/ [Accessed 6th Mar 2017].

[2] 2012 saw the demise of Kodak ...

Mui C. (2012). *How Kodak Failed.* Forbes.

Available at: https://www.forbes.com/sites/chunkamui/2012/01/18/how-kodak-failed/#1c643d446f27 [Accessed 6th Mar 2017].

[3] **The ability to read, control, manage, and influence ...**

Salovey, P. and Mayer, J (1990). *Emotional Intelligence.* Yale University

[4] **In 1996, Harvard Professor Daniel Goleman ...**

Goleman, D.. *Emotional Intelligence.* [blog] Available at: http://www.danielgoleman.info/topics/emotional-intelligence/ [Accessed 6 Mar. 2017]

[5] **Studies on communication by Professor Albert Mehrabian ...**

Mehrabian, A. (1972). *Nonverbal Communication.* Walter De Gruyter Inc.

[6] **Simply the ability to understand and recognize ...**

Goleman, D.. *Emotional Intelligence.* [blog] Available at: http://www.danielgoleman.info/daniel-goleman-how-self-awareness-impacts-your-work/ [Accessed 6 Mar. 2017].

[7] **Heed the words of Brene Brown, ...**

Goodreads.com. *Quotable Quote.* [online] Available at: http://www.goodreads.com/quotes/357565-owning-our-story-can-be-hard-but-not-nearly-as [Accessed 6 Mar. 2017].

[8] **The brain in its present model is about ...**

Bagley, M. (2014). *Quaternary Period: Climate, Animals & Other Facts.* [online] Livescience. Available at: http://www.livescience.com/43151-quaternary-period.html [Accessed 6 Mar. 2017].

[9] **Cortisol is also known as the stress hormone.**

Mayoclinic.com. *Chronic stress puts your health at risk.* [online] Available at: http://www.mayoclinic.org/healthy-lifestyle/stress-management/in-depth/stress/art-20046037 [Accessed 6 Mar. 2017].

[10] **Today's major, non-accident related killers in the US are ...**

Marcus M. B. (2016) *The top 10 leading causes of death in the U.S.* [online] CBS News. Available at: http://www.cbsnews.com/news/the-leading-causes-of-death-in-the-us/ [Accessed 6 Mar. 2017].

[11] **So, the first thing to note ... ["Kubler-Ross Emotional Cycle of Change"]**

wikipedia.org. *Kübler-Ross model.* [online] Available at: https://en.wikipedia.org/wiki/K%C3%BCbler-Ross_model [Accessed 6 Mar. 2017].

[12] **Our brain today has developed what's called ...**

wikipedia.org. *Negativity bias.* [online] Available at: https://en.wikipedia.org/wiki/Negativity_bias [Accessed 6 Mar. 2017].

[13] **We become victims of a syndrome called the "amygdala hijack", ...**

Goleman, D. (1996). *Emotional Intelligence.* 1st ed. London [etc]: Bloombury

[14] **Stephen R Covey found that one ...**

Covey, S. (2015). *The 7 habits of highly effective people.* 1st ed. [United States]: Mango Media.

Chapter 4: How Resilient People Move

[1] **Changes in our level of hormones influence ...**

Integrativepsychiatry.net. *Neurotransmitters.* [online] Available at: http://www.integrativepsychiatry.net/neurotransmitter.html [Accessed 6 Mar. 2017].

[2] **Cortisol (also known as the stress hormone) ...**

Mayoclinic.org. *Stress management.* [online] Available at: http://www.mayoclinic.org/healthy-lifestyle/stress-management/in-depth/stress/art-20046037 [Accessed 6 Mar. 2017].

[3] **We can actually regulate these hormones ...**

Cooper, B. (2013). *The Science Of Posture: Why Sitting Up Straight Makes You Happier And More Productive.* [online] fastcompany. Available at: https://www.fastcompany.com/3021985/work-smart/the-science-of-posture-why-sitting-up-straight-makes-you-happier-and-more-product [Accessed 6 Mar. 2017].

[4] **Studies have shown that breathing incorrectly ...**

Stresscourse.com. *Stress and the Role of Breathing.* [online] Available at: http://stresscourse.tripod.com/id20.html [Accessed 6 Mar. 2017].

[5] **For example, unobtrusive contraction ...**

Carney, D., Cuddy, A. and Yap, A. (2010). Power Posing: Brief Non-verbal Displays Affect Neuroendocrine Levels and Risk Tolerance. *Psychological Science,* [online] p. 3. Available at: http://faculty.missouri.edu/segerti/capstone/powerposing.pdf [Accessed 6 Mar 2017].

[6] **Harvard Business School professor and researcher ...**

TED (2012). *Amy Cuddy: Your body language shapes who you are.* [online]. Available at: http://www.ted.com/talks/amy_cuddy_your_body_language_shapes_who_you_are/transcript?language=en [Accessed 6 Mar. 2017].

[6] **People who *feel* powerful have higher ...**

TED (2012). *Amy Cuddy: Your body language shapes who you are.* [online]. Available at: http://www.ted.com/talks/amy_cuddy_your_

body_language_shapes_who_you_are/transcript?language=en [Accessed 6 Mar. 2017].

[6] **Her research showed that when people adopted ...**

TED (2012). *Amy Cuddy: Your body language shapes who you are.* [online]. Available at: http://www.ted.com/talks/amy_cuddy_your_body_language_shapes_who_you_are/transcript?language=en [Accessed 6 Mar. 2017].

[7] **The act of putting a wide grin ...**

Stevenson, S. (2012). *There's Magic In Your Smile.* [online] Psychology Today. Available at: https://www.psychologytoday.com/blog/cutting-edge-leadership/201206/there-s-magic-in-your-smile [Accessed 6 Mar. 2017].

[7] **Serotonin also acts as a natural pain reliever ...**

Stevenson, S. (2012). *There's Magic In Your Smile.* [online] Psychology Today. Available at: https://www.psychologytoday.com/blog/cutting-edge-leadership/201206/there-s-magic-in-your-smile [Accessed 6 Mar. 2017].

[7] **Scientists and spiritual teachers alike agree ...**

Stevenson, S. (2012). *There's Magic In Your Smile.* [online] Psychology Today. Available at: https://www.psychologytoday.com/blog/cutting-edge-leadership/201206/there-s-magic-in-your-smile [Accessed 6 Mar. 2017].

[8] **Most powerfully, a smile can change your brain.**

Cytowic, R.(2015). *How Facial Botox Changes Your Brain—Literally.* [online] Psychology Today. Available at: https://www.psychologytoday.com/blog/the-fallible-mind/201501/how-facial-botox-changes-your-brain-literally [Accessed 6 Mar 2017].

[7] **A study published in the journal Neuropsychologia reported ...**

Stevenson, S. (2012). *There's Magic In Your Smile.* [online] Psychology Today. Available at: https://www.psychologytoday.com/blog/cutting-edge-leadership/201206/there-s-magic-in-your-smile [Accessed 6 Mar. 2017].

[7] **It also explains the 2011 findings ...**

Stevenson, S. (2012). *There's Magic In Your Smile.* [online] Psychology Today. Available at: https://www.psychologytoday.com/blog/cutting-edge-leadership/201206/there-s-magic-in-your-smile [Accessed 6 Mar. 2017].

[7] **The part of your brain that's responsible for your facial ...**

Stevenson, S. (2012). *There's Magic In Your Smile.* [online] Psychology Today. Available at: https://www.psychologytoday.com/blog/cutting-edge-leadership/201206/there-s-magic-in-your-smile [Accessed 6 Mar. 2017].

[7] **In a Swedish study, subjects were shown pictures ...**

Stevenson, S. (2012). *There's Magic In Your Smile.* [online] Psychology Today. Available at: https://www.psychologytoday.com/blog/cutting-edge-leadership/201206/there-s-magic-in-your-smile [Accessed 6 Mar. 2017].

[8] **Aside from your mental state, smiling ...**

Barrett, S. (2013). *Secrets of your cells.* 1st ed. Boulder, Colo.: Sounds True.

[9] **Exercise plays a key role in the function of our hormones ...**

McCall, P. *8 HORMONES INVOLVED IN EXERCISE.* [Blog] American Council on Exercise. Available at: https://www.acefitness.org/blog/5593/8-hormones-involved-in-exercise [Accessed 6 Mar. 2017].

[10] **Working out releases endorphins, ...**

Webmd.com. Exercise and Depression. [online] Available at: http://www.webmd.com/depression/guide/exercise-depression#1 [Accessed 6 Mar.2017].

[11] **Endorphins produce a sense of happiness ...**

Scheve, T. *Is there a link between exercise and happiness?* [online] Science: How Stuff Works. Available at: http://science.howstuffworks.com/life/exercise-happiness1.htm [Accessed 7 Mar. 2017].

[12] **Everyone needs a different amount of sleep, ...**

Sleepfoundation.org. *HOW MUCH SLEEP DO WE REALLY NEED?*. [online] Available at: https://sleepfoundation.org/how-sleep-works/how-much-sleep-do-we-really-need [Accessed 7 Mar. 2017].

[13] **Tim "4 Hour Work-Week" Ferriss, ...**

Fourhourworkweek. *The 4-Hour WORKWEEK.* [online] Available at: http://fourhourworkweek.com/ [Accessed 7 Mar. 2017].

[14] **As much as 60% of our body weight ...**

The USGS Water Science School. *The water in you.* [online] Available at: https://water.usgs.gov/edu/propertyyou.html [Accessed 7 Mar. 2017].

[14] **The brain and heart are composed of 73% water .....**

The USGS Water Science School. *The water in you.* [online] Available at: https://water.usgs.gov/edu/propertyyou.html [Accessed 7 Mar. 2017].

[15] **Stress, exhaustion and lethargy are often ...**

Norris, R. *Chronic Fatigue Syndrome and Dehydration.* [online] FatigueAnswers. Available at: http://www.fatigueanswers.com/dehydration.html [Accessed 7 Mar. 2017].

[16] **Today, the major illness related ...**

Nichols, H. (2017). *The top 10 leading causes of death in the United States.* [online] MNT. Available at: http://www.medicalnewstoday.com/articles/282929.php [Accessed 7 Mar. 2017].

[17] **These diseases are caused by degeneration of ...**

Karger, L. (2008). Chronic Inflammation and Degenerative Disease. [online] Healthy Beginnings. Available at: http://hbmag.com/chronic-inflammation-degenerative-disease-2/ [Accessed 7 Mar. 2017].

[18] **Fish is among the healthiest foods ...**

Leech, J. *11 Evidence-Based Health Benefits of Eating Fish.* [online] Authority Nutrition. Available at: https://authoritynutrition.com/11-health-benefits-of-fish/ [Accessed 7 Mar.2017].

[19] **For example, in 1948...**

Grover, L. (1994) August Celebration: A Molecule of Hope for a Changing World. Cell Tech; 1st edition

[20] **Another hormone that stimulates growth ...**

Holmes, L. (2014). *7 Reasons Why We Should Be Giving More Hugs.* [online] The Huffington Post. Available at: http://www.huffingtonpost.com/2014/03/27/health-benefits-of-huggin_n_5008616.html [Accessed 7 Mar. 2017].

[21] **Social scientists have for some years now validated ...**

Field, T. (2010). *Touch for socioemotional and physical well-being: A review.* [online] Elsevier. Available at: http://rolfing.nyc/wp-content/uploads/2016/06/Touch-for-socioemotional-and-physical-well-being-A-review.pdf [Accessed 8 Mar. 2017].

[21] **In a study conducted by the Touch Research Institute ...**

Field, T. (2010). *Touch for socioemotional and physical well-being: A review.* [online] Elsevier. Available at: http://rolfing.nyc/wp-content/uploads/2016/06/Touch-for-socioemotional-and-physical-well-being-A-review.pdf [Accessed 8 Mar. 2017].

[22] **I took to heart the advice Amy Cuddy ...**

TED (2012). *Amy Cuddy: Your body language shapes who you are.* [online] Available at: http://www.ted.com/talks/amy_cuddy_your_body_language_shapes_who_you_are/transcript?language=en [Accessed 6 Mar. 2017].

Chapter 5: How Resilient People Talk

[1] **Our self-talk, the choice of words we use ...**

Reach Out. What is self-talk? [online] Available at: http://au.reachout.com/what-is-self-talk [Accessed 8 Mar. 2017].

[2] **Dr John Demartini, another wise philosopher ...**

Demartini, J. (2006). *Count your blessings.* 1st ed. Carlsbad, Calif.: Hay House.

[3] **Resilient people are conscious of their self-talk ...**

Wellbeing Toolkit. *Self talk & resilience.* [online] Available at: http://wellbeingtools.weebly.com/self-talk--resilience.html [Accessed 8 Mar. 2017].

[4] **Chip and Dan Heath, authors of *Made to Stick*- ...**

Heath, C. and Heath, D. (2010). *Made to stick.* 1st ed. New York: Random House.

[5] **In addition, I subscribe to and love the work of Brian Johnson, …**

Optimize with Brian Johnson. *Philosophers Notes.* [online] Available at: https://www.optimize.me/philosophersnotes/ [Accessed 8 Mar. 2017].

Chapter 6: How Resilient People Think

[1] **Using the words of St Augustine, "Pray …**

Brainy Quote. *Saint Augustine Quotes.* [online] Available at: https://www.brainyquote.com/quotes/quotes/s/saintaugus165165.html [Accessed 8 Mar. 2017].

[2] **Optimists are happier, more resilient …**

Conversano, C., Rotondo, A., Lensi, E., Vista, O, Arpone, F. and Reda, M. [2010]. *Optimism and Its Impact on Mental and Physical Well-Being.* [online] Available at: https://www.ncbi.nlm.nih.gov/pmc/articles/PMC2894461/ [Accessed 8 Mar. 2017].

[3] **Whether one is an optimist or pessimist can actually be measured by …**

Centre for confidence. *What is optimism?* [online] Available at: http://www.centreforconfidence.co.uk/pp/overview.php?p=c2lkPTQmdGlkPTAmaWQ9NTU= [Accessed 8 Mar. 2017].

[4] **In 1990, Dr Seligman and his colleagues …**

Dunavold, P. (1997). *Happiness, Hope, and Optimism.* California State University, Northridge. [online] Available at: http://www.csun.edu/~vcpsy00h/students/happy.htm [Accessed 8 Mar. 2017].

[5] **In research done with insurance salespeople …**

Lowman, R. (2002). *The California School of Organizational Studies handbook of organizational consulting psychology.* 1st ed. San Francisco, Calif.: Jossey-Bass.

[6] **Research on humanistic psychology reveals ...**

Kelland, M.. Carl Rogers and Abraham Maslow. Openstax CNX. [online] Available at: http://cnx.org/contents/6xIQ4iAP@1/Carl-Rogers-and-Abraham-Maslow [Accessed 8 Mar. 2017].

[7] **Anthony Robbins, who for the last thirty years ...**

Robbins, T. (2014). *Tony Robbins: 6 Basic Needs That Make Us Tick.* [online] Entrepreneuer. Available at: https://www.entrepreneur.com/article/240441 [Accessed 8 Mar. 2017].

[8] **Abraham Maslow, who studied ...**

McLeod, S. (2016). *Maslow's Hierarchy of Needs.* [online] SimplyPsychology. Available at: http://www.simplypsychology.org/maslow.html [Accessed 8 Mar. 2017].

[9] **In essence, resilient people are learning or growth-oriented ...**

Bauer, Jack J., and Sun W. Park. "Growth is not just for the young: Growth narratives, eudaimonic resilience, and the aging self." *New frontiers in resilient aging: Life-strengths and well-being in late life* (2010): 60-89.

[10] **This reminds me of the story ...**

Instructor. *Struggle is Good!   I Want to Fly!* [online] Available at: http://instructor.mstc.edu/instructor/swallerm/Struggle%20-%20Butterfly.htm [Accessed 8 Mar. 2017].

[11] **This technique is called reframing.**

Changing Minds. *Reframing.* [online] Available at: http://changingminds.org/techniques/general/reframing.htm [Accessed 8 Mar. 2017].

[12] **Michael Jordan was cut from his ...**

Starkes, J. and Ericsson, K. (2003). *Expert performance in sports.* 1st ed. Champaign, IL: Human Kinetics.

[13] **Soichiro Honda was turned down by Toyota Motor Corporation...**

Staff Writers (2010). *Mourners honor Mother Teresa at funeral Mass.* OnlineCollege.Org [online] Available at: http://www.onlinecollege.org/2010/02/16/50-famously-successful-people-who-failed-at-first/ [Accessed 8 Mar. 2017].

[14] **Steve Jobs was fired from the company ...**

Siegel, J. (2011). When Steve Jobs Got Fired By Apple. [online] Available at:

http://abcnews.go.com/Technology/steve-jobs-fire-company/story?id=14683754 [Accessed 8 Mar. 2017].

[15] **Oprah Winfrey was born out of wedlock to ...**

Winfrey, O., Becker, A. and Engelmann, J. (n.d.). *Own it.* 1st ed. Agate Publishing.

[16] **By making this a regular ritual, ...**

Hanson, R. (n.d.). *Hardwiring happiness.* 1st ed. New York: Harmony.

[18] **2 years ago, my niece Rosanne bought ...**

Ames M., Ames D., Ames K., (2014). *Will to Live.* Penguin Books.

[19] **But as the inspirational teacher Brian Tracey says, ...**

Tracy, B. (2010). *Crunch point.* 1st ed. [Hamilton, N.Z.]: Summaries.Com.

Chapter 7: How Resilient People Think

[1] **And then there are folks like Jessica Simpson, ...**

Wikipedia. *Jessica Watson*. [online] Available at: https://en.wikipedia.org/wiki/Jessica_Watson [Accessed 8 Mar. 2017].

[2] **"Great leaders", Simon Sinek says, "start with the *Why*?"**

Sinek, S. (2016). *Start with why*. 1st ed. United States: Joosr Ltd.

[3] **Or how about the guy who was born without hands ...**

Hallowell, B. (2014). *Man Born Without Limbs Delivers Life-Changing Message: 'I'm in Awe, I'm in Shock, I'm Humbled'*. [online] theblaze. [Available at: http://www.theblaze.com/news/2014/06/05/born-with-no-arms-or-legs-he-tried-to-end-his-life-at-age-10-now-hes-inspiring-millions/ [Accessed 8 Mar. 2017].

[4] **Have you watched the real life drama ...**

IMDb. (2011). *127 Hours*. [online]. Available at: http://www.imdb.com/title/tt1542344/ [Accessed 8 Mar. 2017].

[5] **20% of the people in every role in every ...**

Better Explained. *Understanding the Pareto Principle (The 80/20 Rule)*. [online]. Available at: https://betterexplained.com/articles/understanding-the-pareto-principle-the-8020-rule/ [Accessed 8 Mar. 2017].

[6] **Heed the words of Mark Twain, who ...**

BrainyQuote. *Mark Twain Quotes*. [online]. Available at: https://www.brainyquote.com/quotes/quotes/m/marktwain141714.html [Accessed 8 Mar. 201

www.ingramcontent.com/pod-product-compliance
Lightning Source LLC
Chambersburg PA
CBHW071900290426
44110CB00013B/1225